girls! girls! girls!

foreword
by jonathan ross

Is this lethal ninja babe a Deadly China Doll or just Jonathan Ross in disguise? **Left:** Amy Yip and friend from Robotrix get the thumbs up from Jonathan (for two big reasons we suspect)…

I had originally started this introduction with a rather pointless and rambling overview of the past hundred years of cinematic experience, allowing me to speculate that the long hard slog had all been worthwhile now that we could feast our eyes and many of our other senses on the glory that is Eastern action fighting femmes – or Deadly China Dolls as one movie title of this most lip-smackingly enticing genre describes them.

"The whole idea of sexy Chinese girls wearing tight superhero type costumes, fighting and then having sex, is possibly the finest development in the hundred years of cinema history a man could possibly hope for. There's absolutely nothing in these movies that I find anything but joyful"

– Jonathan Ross, Eastern Heroes Video Magazine #2

top 10 traditional fighting femme films DEFINITELY WORTH A VIEW

1 QUEEN BOXER
   aka THE AVENGER
2 HAPKIDO
3 THE TOURNAMENT
4 BROKEN OATH
5 WOMAN AVENGER
6 TWO WONDROUS TIGERS
7 DRAGON INN
8 MASSACRE SURVIVOR
9 VENGEANCE OF A
   SNOWGIRL
10 WOLF DEVIL WOMAN

Judy Lee in Queen Boxer

She's lean, she's keen and she's busting out on the Big Screen!
Kung Fu Mama

But of course our appreciation of high kicking, gun toting, scantily clad Asian babes has nothing to do with any other form of film than their own. To drool over Maggie Cheung, Anita Mui, Amy Yip, Sally Yeh or any one of the other gorgeous and talented women who appear in this feisty fun-fest is more to do with your attitude, whether male or female, to the alluring charm of the young woman in question than it is to do with your appreciation and understanding of the ontology of cinema.

That's not to say that the film sucks. Well, okay, some of them do. But for the most part the gorgeous damsels who are rarely in distress, are just the delectable icing on a thoroughly enjoyable cake. Even after you have removed the lethal chick from the equation of films like *Tiger Cage 2*, *Eastern Condors*, or *Yes Madam* there would still be incredibly exciting slabs of entertainment for you to feast your eyes on.

So, let me get personal if I may for a few moments. I first encountered this rare bird of paradise in Ching Siu Tung's *A Chinese Ghost Story* (1987) where I discovered the haunting beauty of Joey Wong, after which I managed to view a copy of Tsui Hark's *Roboforce*, also known as *I Love Maria*, a movie which I did not find particularly good except for the fact that it had the curvaceous figure of Sally Yeh in the lead. From hereon in I was hooked on the Deadly China Dolls scene. But it wasn't until a few years later that directors who had been making movies themed around blood, honour and revenge realised that these themes could be given a different twist if they came packaged in very high heels, kicking fist to fingernails in very short skirts, or maybe even some closely fitting jogging shorts, or if I can indulge my fantasy even further maybe an evening dress that gets ripped off when the action starts. But I digress, and very pleasant for a moment it was too.

So the bottom line is, if you like kung fu, if you like Heroic Bloodshed, if you like New Wave fantasy films or period dramas or even slightly soppy romances, then how could you possibly not like these movies, even more so when they have placed a scantily clad, beautiful, sexy and tough girl in the lead role? Your Honour, I rest my case.

The Asian fighting female, or the Deadly China Doll, is now as important a chapter in the history of modern Asian cinema as Jackie Chan, or Akira Kurosawa, or, maybe, even Bruce Lee.

Some of you will have bought or stolen this book just for the pictures, and that's okay. In fact, I grudgingly admire your good taste. But I hope you will take time to linger over the excellent words as well as the stunning pictures. Rather like the way you didn't actually get around to reading any of the articles in the very first copy of *Playboy* that you got your mitts on, so too will you one day stop salivating over the photos in this publication and find yourself starting to read the text and when you do, you'll be a man my son.

Jonathan 'Master of Lobster Style Fu' Ross

• Jonathan Ross is one of the UK's best loved TV presenters. His series *The Incredibly Strange Picture Show* ran for two seasons, during which in 1989 he did a special on Jackie Chan. He also highlighted the career of Tsui Hark, and it was this show that brought us the first clips on UK television of Chow Yun Fat. The series also inspired the best-selling book of the same name which was recently revised to include a chapter on Hong Kong cinema.

The Essential Guide to

Rick Baker • Toby Russell
Contributions by Howard Lake • Chris Mercer
Edited by Lisa Baker

PUBLICATIONS

First published in the United Kingdom 1996 by Eastern Heroes Publications,
a subsiduary of Eastern Heroes Ltd.
96 Shaftesbury Avenue, London, W1V 7DH, England.
Copyright © 1996 Eastern Heroes Ltd.

Produced by Rick Baker and Toby Russell
Edited by Lisa Baker.
Contributing material by Howard Lake, Chris Mercer, Jonathan Ross and Tony Rayner.
All text reverts back to the author of the piece.

Design, typesetting, picture origination, additional research (names) by Nick Cairns
at the Eastern Heroes Design Dept (UK), Nottingham.

Printed by Willow Tree Press ,
Arch 268-270, Lancaster Road, London, E11 3EH.

Photographs courtesy of the Baker/Russell Archive.

Special acknowledgement and thanks to the following companies: Golden Harvest, Media
Asia, Win's Film Company, Filmswell International, Golden Princess, Shaw Brothers Studios,
CineMart, Film Bi-Weekly, Made in Hong Kong, Missing in Action, Film Workshop, Wong Jing
Film Productions, ATV, TVB, D&B Films and the many other Hong Kong and Taiwan based
film companies who have helped in the compilation of this book.

Special thanks to the following people: Hilda Lee, Sophia Russell, Alain De la mata, Ricky
Wong, K.K. Cheung, Akin Wong, Lisa Baker, Peggy Lee Schaeffer, the Lau Brothers, Mike
Lee, John Brennan, Laurence Ronson, Rainer Czech, my bank manager, Moon Lee, Yeung
Pan Pan, Maggie Cheung, Yukari Oshima, Michiko Nishiwaki and all the other beautiful
babes that appear in this book. Plus all the guys and girls who champion Hong Kong movies
in America – Oriental Cinema, She Magazine, Hong Kong Connection, without whose
dedication there would be a massive void in our appreciation of Asian cinema.

Front cover image: Chingamy Yau "Naked Killer". Courtesy of M.I.A.

British Library Cataloguing-in-Publication Data
A catalogue record for this book is available from the British Library

ISBN: 1-899252-02-9
First Edition 1996   10 9 8 7 6 5 4 3 2 1

Other Publications from Eastern Heroes:
The Essential Guide to Hong Kong Movies (Publisher: Made in Hong Kong)

The Best of Eastern Heroes (Eastern Heroes Publications. ISBN: 1-899252-01-0)

Eastern Heroes magazine (Eastern Heroes Publications)
Quarterly magazine. Subscription rates from Eastern Heroes,
96 Shaftesbury Ave, London, W1V 7DH, England. Tel: 0171-734-4554

For a complete mail order catalogue of Hong Kong titles available in the UK
write to: Interactive Mail, P.O. Box 30, Hinckley, Leicestershire, LE10 1ZJ, England.
Tel/Fax: 01455-611077 or e-mail at: 106026.553@compuserve.com

Contents

"YOU TALKIN' TO ME?"

Joyce Godenzi and crew, and anyone who can hold a gun

for that matter, make a stand – She shoots Straight

Jackie Chan wants to fumble in Hong Kong in the movie City Hunter

deadly china dolls

a guide to oriental bad girl cinema

Introduction by **Rick Baker**

Deadlier than the male. Yeung Pan Pan gets up to some typical femme fatale acrobatics

The Essential Guide to Deadly China Dolls is a project that has been nurtured for almost three years. The idea was conceived as we were writing our first book, *The Essential Guide to Hong Kong Movies*. It was at that time that Hong Kong cinema was starting to flourish in the UK, and video shops and wholesalers were no longer willing to just settle for Jackie Chan or Bruce Lee titles.

Hong Kong cinema was gaining a new level of respect with the western audience, and distinct genres were emerging, from new wave to Heroic Bloodshed, Category III to modern day action, and above all the femme fatale genre.

There has been such a high level of interest in Hong Kong femme fatale movies that we felt the demand for information about Oriental female stars needed to be addressed. It's been a daunting task,

The gals are all here for The Inspector Wears a Skirt 2

As we all know, girls hunt in packs!
Top: Pink Bomb
Middle: Dreaming the Reality
Bottom: The Virgin Commandos want it now!

though: despite its popularity, experts on the subject are few and far between. For most people it seems to be a case of 'I know what I like' or 'I like what I see'. Some individuals pursue the films of one particular star, while others will buy a film on the title alone and hope it lives up to their expectations. We hope what we have compiled here will pique the interest of everyone who wants to know more about Hong Kong cinema, and that it will serve as a good beginner's guide, as well as a valuable reference tool for the more knowledgeable among you.

Completing this book has certainly expanded my own knowledge of the female stars of the Jade screen, and we have aimed to bring you a well balance study which deals not just with the current crop of stars but also the heroines of yesteryear, when the

Moon Lee, Yukari Oshima, Michiko and Cynthia Khan together at last for Avenging Quartet

A murderous Trio for Angel Enforcers

traditional kung fu film was laying the foundation for today's fast paced femme fatale flicks.

We also have a section on the seductive roles of the Category III stars, who are proving highly popular around the world. With the explosion of female stars in the nineties it's not easy to put a name to every face, but we've tried to include as many as possible, whether their status is cult or just cameo. We hope to revise the book within a couple of years, so before you complain that we've omitted your favourite actress, why not write and we'll see what we can do next time.

Anyway, this project has already spiralled out of control from a profile of action stars in hit movies, to include more serious actresses, erotic starlets and lesser known faces. The time has to come when you say, 'no more!', but we certainly hope it was worth the wait!

I'd like to thank all those who gave us support in this venture and contributed to making it happen, particularly my wife Lisa, Howard Lake, Chris Mercer, our overworked designer/typesetter Nick Cairns who has lived and breathed Asian babes for eight months, Hilda Lee, Sophia Russell and Jonathan Ross. Without these people, myself and Toby would still be working on it!

Chingamy Yau, Sandra Ng, Carrie Ng and Christy Chung get together for Modern Romance

top 20 payrolls of deadly china dolls in 1993

THE YEAR THAT SAW CATEGORY III AND FEMME FATALE ACTION SOARING AT THE BOX OFFICE (10HK$ = £1.00 approx)

Actress	HK Dollars	UK Sterling (£)
Michelle Yeoh	$35,000,000	£3,500,000
Anita Mui	$16,000,000	£1,600,000
Brigitte Lin	$16,000,000	£1,600,000
Joey Wong	$16,000,000	£1,600,000
Gong Li	$15,000,000	£1,500,000
Sally Yeh	$12,000,000	£1,200,000
Chingamy Yau	$10,000,000	£1,000,000
Veronica Yip	$10,000,000	£1,000,000
Maggie Cheung	$10,000,000	£1,000,000
Carina Lau	$10,000,000	£1,000,000
Rosamund Kwan	$10,000,000	£1,000,000
Cheung Man	$8,000,000	£800,000
Michelle Reis	$7,000,000	£700,000
Moon Lee	$6,000,000	£600,000
Cynthia Khan	$6,000,000	£600,000
Sandra Ng	$6,000,000	£600,000
Carrie Ng	$5,000,000	£500,000
Amy Yip	$4,000,000	£400,000
Cathy Chow	$3,500,000	£350,000
Pauline Chan	$2,000,000	£200,000

Source: Affairs Weekly Magazine

top 10 femme fatale flicks to see if you're new to this scene

(NOT NECESSARILY IN THIS ORDER)

1 ANGEL
2 OUTLAW BROTHERS
3 YES MADAM
   aka POLICE ASSASSINS 2
4 THE HEROIC TRIO
5 POLICE ASSASSINS
   aka ROYAL WARRIORS
6 THE BRIDE WITH WHITE HAIR
7 ABOVE THE LAW
8 BLACK CAT
9 QUEEN'S HIGH
10 HOLY WEAPON aka SEVEN MAIDENS

A bevvy of babes in
Holy Weapon, aka
Seven Maidens

NOTES ABOUT DEADLY CHINA DOLLS

i. The filmographies contained within this book are often selective and should not be considered complete. Verifying the entire career of every single actress would be an impossible task as few records exist and the output of the Hong Kong cinema industry is phenomenal. To conduct exhaustive research would have delayed the book indefinitely!

ii. The year of release for each movie has been judged as accurately as possible. Where impossible to confirm, the year will be identified as unknown (?). If the decade is verified but the exact year is uncertain it will appear as (198?). As discrepancies occur in material from the Hong Kong movie industry itself, these discrepancies may be reflected at times.

iii. Most Hong Kong stars have various spellings of their names, depending whether a Cantonese or Mandarin version is used. For consistency, we have kept to the better known versions which we use in *Eastern Heroes* magazine.

While every attempt has been made to ensure the accuracy of all facts, please understand that there is no definitive source of information on this very difficult subject.

Pai Lai Lee!

Little girl, what are you doing out so late at night?

Out to kill you!

Ha! Ha! You're very funny, little girl. Let's sit down and talk a bit. Just answer me, who are you anyway, and what have I done to upset you?

Listen very carefully. I've come here alone all the way to Shanghai Bay just to buy two special coffins. One is for my brother Ma Yung Chen's body.

We fed your brother's body to the fish. And the second coffin?

Either for me or it's for you!

Ha! Ha! You've got it all worked out. However, my dear girl, I think you'd better take some fish from the river back to Shantung with you.

Pai Lai Lee, I've come here to get revenge for my murdered brother and I don't even care if it kills me, but you won't live either!

Queen Boxer

the queen boxers

Angela Mao pulls a shape against Carter Wong in Legendary Strike

text:
Toby Russell

Before the Kung Fu craze hit in the early seventies, the West's preconceived image of the China doll was anything but deadly. A delicate porcelain concubine or a reclining empress were about the limit of the westerner's understanding of the classical Chinese woman. Angela Mao changed all that when she portrayed Bruce Lee's lovely but deadly sister in *Enter the Dragon*. Already a star in the Orient, Angela quickly gained a legion of fans in the west who wanted more of this femme fatale fury.

Fighting females were no strangers to the Chinese, however, who have enjoyed tales of female chivalry for thousands of years. Fables dating back to the Western Han period (206 BC – 23 AD) tell heroic tales of emancipated female knights overcoming enormous odds in the search for justice, honour and love.

The earliest femme fatale stars were the Peking Opera actresses of the Ching Dynasty (1644-1911). The name Do Ma Dan or Wu Dan was given to the actress specializing in military and martial roles. Young girls were sold into the opera, some as young as four, and put through years of horrendous and tortuous exercises which involve acrobatics, juggling, contortion, martial arts including over twenty weaponry skills, singing, dance, mime, make up and knowledge of musical instruments.

It was no wonder that a major Wu Dan star would attract huge publicity and guarantee massive turnouts. They could attarct a hugh fan base – fans would travel far and wide to get a glimpse of their idol's performance. Stars were often mobbed in much the same way a modern pop star is. To be the escort of one of these bewitching female warriors was the desire of every well-to-do professional; warlords and officials particularly enjoyed being in the company of such stardom and much face was gained by being with them. The fascination of dominating these strong women was a huge ego boost for any suitor.

The Wu Dan of today is just as skilful but they do not enjoy the superstar status of opera stars of yesteryear. Probably the last great Wu Dan stars were Angela Mao and Judy Lee, whose stage performances in Taiwan got them recognised by eager movie producers wanting to cash in on their martial talents.

Operas featuring a Wu Dan player in a starring role include the tragic love story *The White Snake*, about an immortal snake who comes to earth and falls in love with a mortal, resulting in much divine mayhem. This tale has been committed to celluloid several times, most recently by Tsui Hark as the film *Green Snake*.

*Giving a Pearl on Rainbow Bridg*e is another martial arts love fable in which a heavenly nymph angers the gods by falling in love with a mortal. Wonder gods Na Cha the Great and Er Lang are despatched to do battle with the young nymph.

Other favourites include *The Woman Warriors of the Yang Family* and *The Lady Sai Hua*, both excerpts from the Sung Dynasty (960-1279) saga *The Yang Generals*.

The martial battles which take place in these operas are set pieces which go far beyond their big screen kung fu movie counterparts and really have to be seen to be believed. The spear kicking in *Rainbow Bridge* is guaranteed to bring an audience to its feet.

With the advent of film it was inevitable

White Snake in battle array, during a performance of the Peking Opera

Yeng Kim Fei – one of the earliest female actresses to gain attention

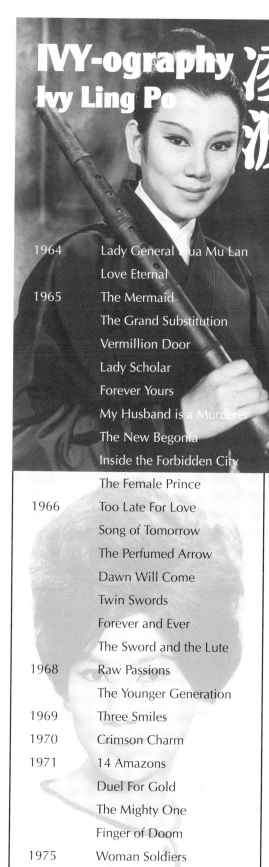

IVY-ography
Ivy Ling Po

凌波

1964	Lady General Hua Mu Lan
	Love Eternal
1965	The Mermaid
	The Grand Substitution
	Vermillion Door
	Lady Scholar
	Forever Yours
	My Husband is a Murderer
	The New Begonia
	Inside the Forbidden City
	The Female Prince
1966	Too Late For Love
	Song of Tomorrow
	The Perfumed Arrow
	Dawn Will Come
	Twin Swords
	Forever and Ever
	The Sword and the Lute
1968	Raw Passions
	The Younger Generation
1969	Three Smiles
1970	Crimson Charm
1971	14 Amazons
	Duel For Gold
	The Mighty One
	Finger of Doom
1975	Woman Soldiers

that the opera stars would fizzle out. The figure of the swordswoman is perhaps the most charismatic in Chinese cinema, mostly alone and taking on the appearance of a young male scholar, or sometimes handicapped. This outwardly incapable appearance only enhances the beauty of the action. The plots of the sword films are more tragic than heroic, with either the heroine or

Chan Bo Chu

the knight she loves perishing in the final reel. The first big star in the black and white operatic Cantonese films was Yeng Kim Fai, a Cantonese opera singer whose pictures have been the bread and butter of Hong Kong audiences for the last six decades, with constant late night reruns. One of Yeng's films was the inspiration for *God of Gamblers*, and she even appeared opposite an adolescent Bruce Lee in *We Owe It To Our Children*, in which she tries to introduce the young master to the world of literature.

Ivy Ling Po with Bruce Lee

As popular but not of operatic background was Chan Bo Chu, who could be compared to Bruce Lee in terms of popularity in Hong Kong. Ivy Ling Po is another female star of yesteryear with a huge legion of fans.

Double guns long before John Woo. Chan Bo Chu

The premier real fighting starlet to emerge from Hong Kong was a young Shanghainese dancer named Cheng Pei Pei, who after completing a six month actors' training course at the Shaw Brothers studio was selected by director King

陳寶珠

Cheng Pei Pei

Hu to play the lead role in his 1965 production *Come Drink With Me*. Using a pair of deadly daggers and with the aid of a drunken swordsman, superbly portrayed by Yue Hwa, she manages to rescue her kidnapped brother from a gang of tyrants headed by the dastardly Chan Hung Lieh. Great atmosphere and delicate fight sequences and gimmickry made it an unforgettable film. Also the fact that Golden Swallow was the only female in the film apart from the beggar children helped enforce the charisma and the mystery of the lone swordswoman against the odds in a world of male rogues and knights. The film won both box office success and worldwide critical acclaim for director and star alike. Cheng Pei Pei was to reprise her role as Golden Swallow in Chang Cheh's film of the same name, released in the west as *Girl With the Thunderbolt Kick* (1969).

Director Lo Wei was also captivated by Cheng Pei Pei's charisma and cast her in numerous pictures including the poisonously atmospheric *Dragon Swamp* (1967), the chilly *Shadow Whip* in which she uses a six foot bullwhip as her weapon of choice, the overindulgent and slow *Raw Courage* and last but by no means least, the Golden Harvest classic *Kung Fu Girl* in which she broke the mould of the swordswoman and opted for the role of an emancipated female fist fighter taking on Japanese aggressors in war torn China. Besides good fight scenes and a run of the mill storyline the picture has two interesting factors. The first is the unusual choice of top Japanese actor Shishido Jo as male lead, an extraordinary looking individual whose performance as the oddball hitman in the black and white Japanese classic *Branded to Kill* remains one of the highlights of Japanese cinematic history. The second is the beginning of a long lasting collaboration between Jackie Chan (who had a supporting role as a

This page:

The many faces of Chan Bo Chu

Chan Bo Chu, the first deadly angel

PEI PEI-ography
Cheng Pei Pei

1964	Lovers' Rock
	Last Woman of Shang
1965	Come Drink With Me
	The Lotus Lamp
	Dragon Creek
	Song of Orchid Island
	Brothers 5
	Blue Skies
1967	Dragon Swamp
1968	That Fiery Girl
	Lady of Steel
	Lady Hermit
	Golden Sword
	Raw Courage
	The Jade Raksha
	The Flying Dagger
1969	Golden Swallow aka Girl With the Thunderbolt Kick
	Kung Fu Girl
	Whiplash
	Operation Lipstick
1971	Shadow Whip
1980	Virgin Commandos
1989	Painted Faces
1994	The Gods Must Be Crazy 3

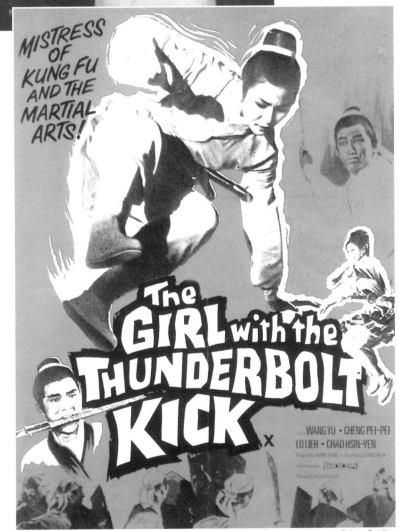

Girl With the Thunderbolt Kick, aka Golden Swallow

1993	Flirting Scholar
1996	How to Meet the Lucky Stars

LI-ography
Li Ching

李菁

Li Ching and David Chiang in New One Armed Swordsman

Li Ching in Vengeance of a Snowgirl

Japanese thug) and Lo Wei. Cheng Pei Pei's career fizzled out shortly after this picture. She chose only to appear in the odd film which took her fancy, *Virgin Commandos* being one example. Recently Cheng Pei Pei has returned to the big screen in Alex Law's *Painted Faces*, in which she played the renowned Peking Opera teacher and star Fan Kok Fa, and even more recently as a high flying, foul mouthed matriarch in the Chow Sing Chi comic classic *Flirting Scholar*.

Cheng Pei Pei's contemporaries who shared the 1960s swashbuckling limelight include Li Ching, a native Cantonese filled with innocence and charm. She captivated audiences with her touching performance as the young crippled girl who travels far and wide to find a cure for her infirmity, only to unselfishly sacrifice herself for the man she loves in *Vengeance of a Snow Girl*. Without a doubt this is Lo Wei's masterpiece, based upon the plot of the opera *Pearl at Rainbow Bridge* but substituting the evil clan for the heavenly deities. Chang Cheh was also won over by Li Ching's charm and cast her opposite a

Vengeance of a Snowgirl

debonaire Ti Lung in the tragic swashbuckler *King Eagle*, and as David Chiang's admirer in the world renowned classic *New One Armed Swordsman*. Li Ching turned to producing in the late seventies, including the rare *Snake Deadly Act*.

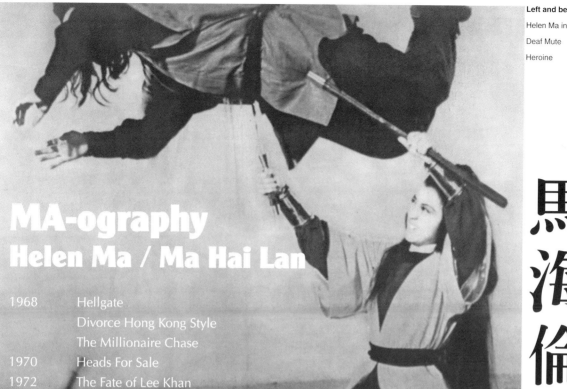

MA-ography
Helen Ma / Ma Hai Lan

1968	Hellgate
	Divorce Hong Kong Style
	The Millionaire Chase
1970	Heads For Sale
1972	The Fate of Lee Khan
	Deaf Mute Heroine
1973	Back Alley Princess
	The Showdown

馬
海
倫

Another swordplay classic which also features a handicapped heroine is Wu Ma's *Deaf Mute Heroine*. Ex-Shaw starlet Helen Ma stars as a beautiful deaf mute swordswoman who uses mirrors in her wristbands to act as her ears. After stealing a consignment of pearls for no other motive but personal gain (a masterfully shot title sequence describes this bloody episode) she becomes the prey of gangsters far and wide. Mortally wounded in an ambush, she finds sanctuary with a kind and simple man with whom she falls in love. Soon her enemies catch up with her and the slaughter continues. Again the plot has a lot in common with *Love of the White Snake*. A wicked woman falls in love with a kind man in the hope she will improve herself. The classically beautiful Helen Ma has never looked better before or since and this remains one of the high points in both her career and the femme fatale genre.

Two other Shaw Brothers starlets who have made a contribution to the genre are Chiao Chiao and Shih Szu. Chiao Chiao will best be remembered as the cute pouting wife of the One Armed Swordsman. In fact the chemistry between Wang Yu and Chiao Chiao worked so well that they were coupled together in

Left:

Chiao Chiao

portrait

CHIAO-ography
Chiao Chiao

焦姣

Chiao Chiao fools around with Wang Yu on the set of One Armed Swordsman

Above:

Chiao Chiao on set with Wang Yu in One Armed Swordsman

pictures even after they left the Shaw Brothers. But Chiao Chiao is a swordswoman in her own right and proved it in the light-hearted swashbuckling classic *Heads For Sale* (1969), in which she rescues her tormented lover from a dastardly clan. She outwits all and sundry with some clever ploys including the selling of severed heads! Shih Szu started working at the Shaw Brothers studio when she was just fifteen and was chosen by the studio executives to fill the shoes of Cheng Pei Pei, who although only in her twenties was considered too old to play a desirable swordswoman. Shih Szu's beauty queen looks and tremendous fighting ability won over the hearts of moviegoers instantly and after initially supporting Cheng Pei Pei she soon knocked her off the top spot with pictures like *The Rescue, Crimson Charm* and *Lady Hermit* and as the poisonous dragon in *Young Avenger*. Western audiences got a taste of Shih Szu when she appeared alongside

Shih Szu portrait

Shih Szu in Massacre Survivor

SZU-ography
Shih Szu

1970   Crimson Charm
1971   The Iron Bow
         Lady of the Law
         Young Avenger
         Lady Hermit
         Swift Knight
         The Rescue
1972   The Pirate
1973   The Escape
1974   Superman of the Orient
         Shadow Boxer
         Ghost Eyes
         Legend of the Seven
             Golden Vampires
1975   Marco Polo
         Flying Guillotine 2
         The Hustlers
         Temperament of Life
1976   Drug Connection
         Naval Commandos
1977   Jade Tiger
         Clan of Amazons
         Magic Blade
1978   Deadly Breaking Sword
         Avenging Eagle
1979   Precious Jade
         The Heroes
         The Revenger
         Massacre Survivor
         Relentless Broken Sword
         Night of the Assassin
1980   Chinese Magic
         A Deadly Secret
1981   Lone Ninja Warrior
             aka 13 Moon Sword
         Kung Fu Emperor

Shih Szu in The Pirate

思
施

took her as an honorary disciple and cast her in several of his pictures, the most memorable role being the wife of famed Shaolin boxer Hung Shi Kwan in *Executioners From Shaolin*. Kung fu superstar Jackie Chan also requested her to play the skirt kung fu expert in his box office smash *Young Master*.

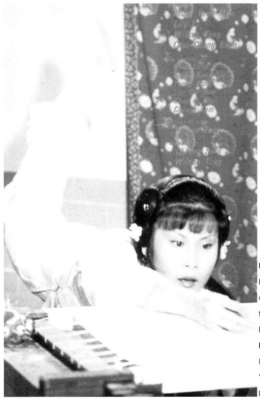

Left:
Lilly Lee
demonstrates
the swing style in
Daggers 8
Below:
Lilly and Meng
Yuan Man in
Daggers 8

Hammer supremo Peter Cushing in *Legend of the Seven Golden Vampires*.

   Another Shaws crossover actress who played opposite Cushing in a Shaws/Hammer co-production, *Shatter*, was the multi-faceted Lilly Lee. She is still acting today and has been in hundreds of movies. Her acting range is vast to say the least, whether portraying a naive swordswoman as in *Shadow Girl*, a sexy gangster's moll as in Chang Cheh's *Four Riders*, or dominating the scene as a flashy kung fu fighter as in *The Loot*. Lilly Lee's kung fu master Lau Kar Leung was so taken with her martial ability and gift for acting that he

LILLY-ography
Lilly Lee / Lee Li Li

李麗麗

1968	Spring Blossom	1977	Shaolin Mantis
	Enchanted Chamber		Jade Tiger
	That Fiery Girl		Soul of Sword
1969	Wandering Swordsman		My Blade My Life
1970	Love Song Over the Sea	1978	One Foot Crane
	The Heroic Ones		Shaolin Abbot
	Tropicana Interlude		Deadly Breaking Sword
1971	Shadow Girl		Clan Feuds
	Have Sword Will Travel	1979	Daggers 8
	Six Assassins		The Challenger
1972	Four Riders		The Crazy Couple
	Champions of Champions	1980	The Loot
1973	The Delinquent		Young Master
	Friends	1982	Mission to Kill
	Nobody's Son		Eight Diagram Pole Fighters
1974	Iron Bodyguard		Long Road to Gallantry
	Rivals of Kung Fu	1983	Dreadnaught
	Scandal		I'll Finally Knock You
1975	Shatter		Down Dad
	Black Magic	1984	Disciples of the
	Oily Maniac		36th Chamber
1976	Executioners From Shaolin		
	Black Magic 2:		
	Revenge of the Zombies		

Below: Lilly Lee in Four Riders, also known as Hellfighters of the East, with David Chiang

Right: Lilly Lee with Tsui Siu Keung and David Chiang in The Challenger

Lilly Lee poses with Jackie Chan in this rare shot

But rising above all the actresses of the seventies are three kung fu queens who will be no strangers to anyone even remotely interested in the genre – the first and foremost being Angela Mao Ying. She was born on September 20, 1950, the third phoenix in a family of seven (her younger brother Mao Tao has also appeared in well over 200 films). When she was five she was enrolled into Taiwan's prestigious Fu Shing opera school. Among her tiny classmates were Chang Yi, James Tien, Lee Yi Min, Charlie Chin and Judy Lee.

Angela quickly picked up the different skills she was taught and blossomed into a fine martial actress and singer. She was rewarded by her teachers with much sought after warrior roles such as White Snake and Lady Sai Hua. When she was twelve she went on tour with the troupe to the US and Japan, mesmerising audiences wherever she appeared.

The following year, she joined the elite Hai Kwang opera troupe, a company renowned for intense training, strict discipline and high performance acrobatics. Truth be known, several members of this company have either died, been crippled for life or gone mad due to the high level of training. But good training pays off and in 1969 Angela's prowess caught the eye of Golden Harvest ace director Huang Feng, who signed her up and cast her in his film *Angry River*. She uses her daring and consummate swordplay to overcome demons and villains as she searches for a magical antidote to cure her sick father. Once again

the plot is lifted from ancient Chinese folklore and the batting order of the fight sequences is arranged pretty much as they would be on stage.

Angela remained with Golden Harvest for five more years, starring in hit after hit. The two films which won her a huge legion of fans in the west were *Lady Whirlwind* (aka *Deep Thrust*, *Hand of Death*) and *Hapkido*, in which she adapted empty hand and kicking techniques in place of traditional weapons. The antagonists too were different. Instead of traditional Chinese villains, imperialist Japanese were now the nemesis of choice,

Angela Mao kicks out in The Damned

Angela gives Ng Kun Lung a good telling off in Snake Deadly Act

Angela Mao attempts her own stunts in The Angry River

Angela Mao off set in The Opium Trail, aka Deadly China Doll

Following *Hapkido*, Angela starred in the lost classic *Opium Trail* (aka *Deadly China Doll*) produced by *Rambo* producer Andrew Vajana. Other Golden Harvest classics she appeared in were *The Fate of Lee Khan*, directed by King Hu, in which she plays a waitress at an inn of intrigue, and *Stoner*, a modern day action piece which sees her teaming up with James Bond star George Lazenby to crack a drug syndicate, the high point of which is a ten minute leg exchange finalé with Hwang In Shik. A second outing with Lazenby, *Queen's Ransom* aka *Operation Regina*, took Angela to the golden

Angela Mao in Scorching Sun, Fierce Wind, Wild Fire

using Japanese bushido to discredit Chinese and Korean martial arts.

So proficient were Angela's empty hand techniques that audiences and reporters believed that she was indeed a Hapkido black belt. Even real life Hapkido master Hwang In Shik said of her, "She was the most intelligent student I ever had. She picked up the art of Hapkido overnight, so we awarded her an honorary black belt."

ANGELA-ography

Angela Mao Ying

茅瑛

1970	The Angry River
1971	Invincible 8
	Thunderbolt
1972	Hapkido
	Lady Whirlwind
	The Fate of Lee Khan
1973	When Taekwando Strikes
	Enter the Dragon
1974	The Association
	The Tournament
	Deadly China Doll aka The Opium Trail
	Naughty Naughty
1975	Stoner
	Operation Regina aka Queen's Ransom
	The Himalayan
1977	Broken Oath
	Revenge of Kung Fu Mao
	Lady Constables
	Swift Shaolin Boxer
	Two Great Cavaliers
	Scorching Sun, Fierce Wind, Wild Fire
	Duel With the Devils
	The Damned
1978	Legendary Strike
	Moonlight Sword Jade Lion
1979	Dance of Death
1980	Devil's Dynamite
	Giant of Casino
1988	Witch's Curse

Three the Hard Way, with Angela Mao, Chen Sing and the legendary Northern Leg John Liu

Top:
Angela Mao
and Carter Wong
in Deadly
China Doll

Middle:
Jackie Chan
choreographs
Angela Mao on
the set of
Dance of Death

Bottom:
Angela Mao holds
her own in
Hapkido

triangle and saw her take up firearms for the first time in order to foil an assassination attempt on Queen Elizabeth II. Co-stars in this extravaganza include Jimmy Wang Yu, Charles Heung, Betty Ting Pei and Her Majesty the Queen!

As the seventies moved ahead, so were the fight scenes updated. *The Himalayan*, choreographed by Samo Hung, saw Angela match kicks and hands with 'Flash Legs' Tan Tao Liang and kung fu strong man Chan Sing in a battle that remains a screen classic to this day.

Angela's last film for Golden Harvest was *Broken Oath*, directed by Korean director Cheng Chang Ho, the man who brought the world *King Boxer*. Angela is given the chance to bring to the screen all of her talents in her quest for vengeance against her mother's killers, a simple storyline lifted by beautifully choreographed fight sequences by Yuen Woo Ping. There is also the added attraction of Bruce Liang's fancy footwork.

Angela Mao tries out the poles with Wilson Tong in The Tournament

Mean and moody, with James Tien in Invincible 8

On leaving Golden Harvest, Angela moved back to Taiwan. After a short rest from filming due to injury and family commitments, she stepped back in front of the lens in several medium budget features. Among the better ones were *Revenge of Kung Fu Mao*, *Moonlight Sword and Jade Lion* and *The Damned*, all of which co-starred Taiwan's resident matinee idol of the seventies, Wong Tao.

The unusual pairing of Angela with John Liu in the classic *Two Great Cavaliers* proved to be terrific chemistry and the film remains one of Angela's best Taiwanese efforts. Her two collaborations with Taiwan's other leg exponent, Tan Tao Liang – *Scorching Sun, Fierce Wind, Wild Fire* and *The Duel With the Devils* – were also competent works but lacked the power and imagination needed in a stagnating genre.

Towards the end of the seventies Angela was chosen by Jackie Chan's assistant director Chen Chi Hwa to star in *Dance of Death*, a femme fatale cash-in on the then popular Jackie Chan kung fu comedy formula. Despite an attractive advertising campaign depicting

Angela takes on Fong Hak An's deadly fan techniques in Snake Deadly Act

Stoner

Angela Mao demonstrates hapkido in Stoner

Hapkido

Angela Mao gives a salute in Stoner

A rare shot of Angela Mao
showing her arms

Jackie as the martial art choreographer, which of course he wasn't, the film, although appreciated by fans, did little at the box office. It was to be Angela's last kung fu film. She did appear in some Taiwanese gambling films, among them *Giant of Casino* and *Devil's Dynamite*, both starring Wong Kwan Hsiung. The last 35mm production Angela appeared in was *Witch's Curse*, a low budget Taiwan horror flick in which she plays a wandering spirit. Currently she divides her time between New York and Taiwan, and has no plans for returning to the big screen.

Another actress from the Fu Shing opera school, and a classmate of Angela Mao, is Chia Ling, also known as Judy Lee. Like Angela, she was an exceptionally gifted stage performer, who even performed male martial roles. Her operatic martial endeavours caught the eye of movie star and producer/director Yeung Kwan, who cast her in his production *The Avenger*, retitled *Queen Boxer* in the US. The story unfolds where *Boxer From Shantung* left off. Ma Yung Chen is killed by Boss Pai and his young sister arrives in Shanghai to settle the score. Shot in eighteen days, the picture was a hit due to the breathtaking tour de

force performance of Judy Lee in the main role. As Ma's sister, she singlehandedly takes on the might of Boss Pai's horrendous army of waterfront killers, and on top of that the

Judy Lee in Unique Lama

JUDY-ography

Judy Lee / Chia Ling / Charline Liu

嘉凌

1972	The Avenger aka Queen Boxer	1977	Ten Brothers of Shaolin
1973	Escape		Glory Sword aka Imperial Sword
	Mystery		Heroine Kam Lian Chu
1974	Girl Called Iron Phoenix		Fists of Dragon
1975	Female Chivalry		Eighteen Swirling Riders
	Female Chivalry 2		Unique Lama
	The Supergirl of Kung Fu		Deadly Confrontation
	Behind Enemy Lines		Ming Patriots
	Sunset in the Forbidden City		Going With the Moon
	Woman Soldiers		Deadly Rivalry
1976	Story in the Temple of the Red Lily	1978	Spring Wind
	Great Hunter		Shaolin Invincibles
	Legend of Mother Goddess		Iron Swallow
	Lantern Street		Revenge of a Shaolin Kid
	Thousand Mile Escort		Hero Tattooed With A Dragon
	Assassin		Revengeful Swordswoman
	Lady Karate aka Spy Ring Kokurykai		Lady Constables
	Fierce Fist		Tough Guy
	Seven Spirit Pagoda	1979	Crane Fighter
1977	Chivalrous Inn		Gone With Honour
	Eight Masters		Thirteen Evil Bandits
	Blazing Temple		

dreaded Axe Gang. The action, shot in long sweeping takes, is spellbinding. Judy gracefully and mercilessly despatches her enemies and seems to relish the very act of working herself up into a possessed frenzy, coming across on screen as totally believeable.

The movie was completed under budget and in time for its immediate release against three other pictures depicting a similar story. "We were competing against three other movies which had the same theme. Although we shot the film in just eighteen days our picture did the best box office," says Judy.

Indeed Judy Lee was so good in the role that the movie producer and co-star Yeung Kwan cast her in his next picture, *The Escape*. Her performance earned her the much coveted Golden Horse award. Judy made over sixty pictures in Taiwan, also shooting one or two in Hong Kong. Her most prominent works are *Queen Boxer*, *The Escape*, *Iron Swallow* and *Female Chivalry*, in which she plays Iron Phoenix, an intrepid detective often dressed as a man. The role was reprised for a further three pictures. *The Crane Fighter*,

Unique Lama

This page: Judy Lee photo showcase

Girl Called
Iron Phoenix

Unique Lama

This page The many faces of Judy Lee

Top: Iron Swallow

Middle: Judy Lee on set

Above: Judy Lee takes on the Peking Opera for The Escape

Right Centre: Judy Lee in the nineties, at work in her travel agent business

Bottom Right: Eight Masters

嘉凌

Girl Called Iron Phoenix

Judy Lee in Chivalrous Inn, directed by David Lin

Both Angela Mao and Judy Lee seem to be very conservative women and have never shown so much as a bare shoulder on the screen. A passionate snog with the male lead is totally out of the question. But then again, when you're wielding a pair of double knives or a staff and kicking ass, who cares? Judy Lee retired from the film world in the early eighties. She currently resides in Los Angeles where she spends her time between her family and her travel agency.

The third and possibly most renowned of the three Taiwanese movie queens is the feisty Polly Shang Kwan Ling Fong. Born on October 10, 1949, she graduated from high school and enroled into the United Film Corp in Taipei in 1966. The following year she was given the chance to star in King Hu's classic *Dragon Inn*, in which she portrayed a young patriot helping to quash the rule of the mighty eunuchs.

After completing the role, Polly devoted the next year to martial arts training. She holds black belts in judo and karate and is a

Polly Shang Kwan Ling Fong in an early publicity shot

Polly Shang Kwan challenges Phillip Kao in The Eighteen Jade Arhats

another classic production from young entrepreneur and star Raymond Liu, showcased her flair for classical shape pulling, demonstrating the crane style. It also stretched her acting ability a little further than normal. In most cases her acting is somewhat one-dimensional and childish, with the exception of the two big budget patriotic, pro-nationalist war pictures *Spring Wind* and *Gone With Honour*, where some emotional depth is explored.

POLLY-ography
Polly Shang Kwan Ling Fong

上官靈鳳

	1976	Seven To One
		Adventure At Shaolin
		Shaolin Kids
		Shaolin Death Squads
		Heroine Kam Lian Chu
		Heroes in the Late Ming Dynasty
		Tiger Cliff
1967	Dragon Inn	Seven Indignant Killers
1968	The Swordsman of	The Great Hero
	All Swordsmen	1977 Rebel of Shaolin
1970	Ghostly Face	Immortal Warriors
	Black Belt Hero	Fight For Shaolin Tamo Systique
1972	Back Alley Princess	1969 Brave and Evil
	Crazy Boys in Hong Kong	Last Battle of Yang Chow
1973	Chinatown Capers	Return of the Eighteen Bronze Men
	Ming Patriots	General Stone
	The Rangers	Mysterious Heroes
1974	Empress Dowager's Agate Vase	Ninety Nine Cycling Sword
	The Venturer	aka Lung Wei Village
1975	Judicial Sword	Eighteen Jade Arhats
	Vigilantes	Kam Sha Yeh
	Crazy Guy	Green Dragon Inn
	Gathering of Heroes	The Traitorious
	A Girl Called Tigress	Invincible Super Guy
	Great Hero	Crazy Boys in Hong Kong
	Eighteen Bronze Men	1978 Super Dragon
	Bruce and Kung Fu Girls	Zodiac Fighters
	Behind Enemy Lines	Red Phoenix
		Revenge of Kung Fu Dragon

36 • *the essential guide to deadly china dolls*

Polly Shang Kwan
with Chang Yi
in The Traitorious

Polly Shang Kwan with Chang Yi in The Traitorious

Fight For
Shaolin
Tamo
Systique

second degree black belt in taekwando. In 1970 she co-starred with Jimmy Wang Yu in the raw classic *Brave and Evil,* as a young karate mistress.

The following year took her to the mystic island of Bali to shoot an adventure film, *The Ghostly Face.* Great sets and costumes plus a nifty musical score helped secure good box office receipts for this off-beat movie.

In 1972 Polly won the Golden Horse award for her performance in the Golden Harvest film *Back Alley Princess,* in which she played a little boy called Pepper who turns out to be a girl, much to the disappointment of Angela Mao, who had fallen for the little rascal. Great fights and comedy made the film a

Polly Shang Kwan lashes out in The Traitorious

Heroine Kam Lian Chu

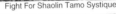
Fight For Shaolin Tamo Systique

A Girl Called Tigress

A Girl Called Tigress

Shaolin
Death
Squad

huge success all over the world, and a sequel, *Chinatown Capers*, followed. This was shot in San Francisco and co-starred Sam Hui, who sings a couple of great numbers, Sylvia Chang and a cameo from Wong Tao.

Like Judy Lee, Polly made over sixty films

漢羅玉八十

THE EIGHTEEN JADE ARHATS

and has appeared in martial TV dramas. But what separates Polly from Angela and Judy is that her approach is far more flamboyant and in many cases outright silly, but always gutsy. She is a true professional who will wear bizarre, skimpy costumes, fight on stilts, be chased by flying sharks, rubber octopi and fight with ghosts, fishmen, flying kite men, bronze men, monks – you name it, she's fought with it! She also made an Italian comedy with the Crazy Boys and generally appears to be having a great time.

Polly made many pictures with Carter Wong. Many thought they would marry but Polly married an American naval officer,

Zodiac Fighters, where lobster style takes on a new meaning

Fight For
Shaolin Tamo
Systique

Chinese
Vengeance

Mysterious Heroes

whom she recently divorced, going on to
marry the son of Taiwanese movie director
Tyrone Hsu. Sadly she retired from shooting
in 1980 with the *Sea Dragon Goddess*, which
co-starred Flash Legs Tan Tao Liang as a white
haired villain. Her exit from films marked the
end of the era of the kung fu queens, an era to
which Polly contributed so much. From its
beginnings in the sixties right through to the
end, she gave it all she had, one hundred
percent. The Chinese had a saying in the
seventies, "The Dragon is Bruce Lee, the
phoenix is Polly Shang Kwan Ling Fong."

Hong Kong has its share of kung fu queens.
First up is Yeung Pan Pan. Of Shanghainese
and Szechuanese descent, Pan Pan started
training when she was four. She persuaded

her mother to let her take lessons at the Fan Kok Fa opera academy. Unlike her classmates Tung Wei, Lam Ching Ying, John Lone and Meng Hoi, Pan Pan had to pay for her lessons since her mother would not let her be a full time student there. Pan Pan loved every minute of her training and learnt many different disciplines while there: "The master would invite many different kung fu teachers to stay in the school and we would learn rare and useful forms of kung fu and acrobatics from them. My mother made me leave the school after two years of training and sent me to study at a proper school.

"Later I studied many different forms of combat from many top masters, including Lee Kwan Hung of Choy Lay Fatt kung fu, Dan Inosanto of jeet kune do fame, western boxing from John Ladawski and karate from Bruce Leung."

In 1978 Pan Pan joined the maverick film company Goldig Films: "Originally I was to

PAN PAN-ography

Yeung Pan Pan

楊盼盼

1978	Kung Fu Master Called Drunk Cat
	Duel to the Death
1979-80	Two Wondrous Tigers
	Story of Drunken Master
1981	Return of the Deadly Blade
	Lion vs Lion
	Kid From Kwang Tung
1981-85	Stunt Women (TV)
	Legend of Condor Heroes (TV)
	Yang Women Warriors (TV)
1990	Angel Enforcers
	Princess Madam
1992	Angel Terminators 2
	Deadly Target
1995	Angel on Fire

This page:

Photo

showcase from

Two Wondrous

Tigers

that time they called me Lady Jackie Chan."

Pan Pan also made two tremendous films at the Shaw Brothers studio, *Lion vs Lion* and the Hwang Jan Lee classic *Kid From Kwang Tung*. Pan Pan is more renowned for her TV appearances in series like *Stunt Women, Legend of Condor Heroes* and *Yang Women Warriors*. One of her trademarks was her annual appearance on Hong Kong's answer to the telethon, in which she would perform feats of tremendous

shave my head and make a female version of *The 36th Chamber of Shaolin*, but the boss, Alex Gouw, said if I shaved my head I could only make one film, so we cancelled the project and started shooting *Kung Fu Master Named Drunk Cat*, followed by *Duel of the Seven Tigers* and *Two Wondrous Tigers*. At

daring including tightrope, unicycle, plate spinning and being fired out of a cannon.

Pan Pan also proved herself a worthy player in the modern day genre, with tour de force performances in the action packed *Angel Terminators* and the Godfrey Ho classic *Angel Enforcers*. Currently she spends her time between housework, looking after her young daughter, and the movie set. Not bad going for a kung fu tomboy.

Yuen Siu Tien instructs Yeung Pan Pan in Legend of the Drunken Master

Yeung Pan Pan, as acrobatic as ever in Angel Engforcers

It wasn't long before Taiwanese maverick producer/director Lee Tso Nam came up with a Taiwanese version of a Lady Jackie Chan. The lovely, leggy Hsia Kwan Lee is a graduate from the Lu Kwang Opera Troupe and her fellow classmates were Venoms Lu Feng and Ching Tien Chee.

After appearing in a couple of low budget swordplay films, Hsia was given a choice role in Lee Tso Nam's *Shaolin Invincible Sticks*, where she portrays a young staff fighting damsel in distress whose fate is saved by the debonair Wong Tao. So impressed was Lee with Hsia's on-screen charisma and skill that he devised a script for her alone. *Woman Avenger* (also known as *Fatal Claws, Deadly Strikes* in the UK) remains one of the femme fatale classics of the late seventies. The story borrows heavily from the British produced spaghetti western *Hannie Calder*. After a gruesome gang rape and witnessing the murder of her husband before her eyes, Hsia's lust for vengeance has her learning a pot pourri of kung fu styles. One by one she dispatches her foes in a series of beautifully choreographed fight scenes in which she uses double sticks, dragon fist and a series of deadly kicks. The end duel with the film's choreographer Pang Gang remains one of the classic femme fatale duels filmed as Pang Gang literally hurtles himself at the woman avenger, who defeats this man-made typhoon with the upside down monkey style.

Lee Tso Nam was so pleased with the film that he cast Hsia Kwan Lee and Pang Gang in his next project *The Leg Fighters*, in which

Left:

Woman Avenger

Below:

Hsia Kwan Lee
versus Jimmy Lee
in Shaolin
Invincible Sticks

夏光莉

HSIA-ography
Hsia Kwan Lee

1978   Shaolin Invincible Sticks

Deadly Secret

The Leg Fighters

1979   Woman Avenger

The Butterfly Murders

1980   Virgin Commandos

1982   Zu: Warriors From the Magic Mountain

Hsia plays the spoilt kicking student of Flash
Legs Tan. After rigorous training the Leg Duo
manage to overcome Pang Gang's 18 Bird
Forms.

Hsia Kwan Lee has since appeared in *Virgin
Commandos* for Lee Tso Nam, followed by
two films for Tsui Hark – *Butterfly Murders*,
where she was one of the leaders of the
Mountain Gang, and the classic *Zu: Warriors
From the Magic Mountain*, as the lieutenant
to Brigitte Lin. Hsia has also appeared in
hours and hours of TV/video productions
from Taiwan where she currently resides.
Sadly movie roles are few and far between
nowadays, due to the heavy dominance of
Hollywood rubbish on Asian cable and movie
screens.

Shaolin
Invincible
Sticks

HUI YING HUNG

惠英紅

Main picture: Hui Ying Hung in a sultry glamour pose

Inset: Hui Ying Hung on the cover of the very first edition of Southern Screen

the lady is the boss...

Auntie with the lethal three section staff in Clan of the White Lotus

hui ying hung

Long Road
to Gallantry

Auntie
poses in
Naughty
Boys

Hui Ying
Hung was born in
1960, the youngest child of
the family, which also
included future Shaw
Brothers star Hui Tien Chi
(*Five Superfighters*, *Gang
Masters*). Unlike her

text:
Chris Mercer

brother and two sisters, who were sent to
Peking Opera school, Hui Ying Hung
remained with her mother at home, though
she managed to pick up a few tricks during
her elder siblings' infrequent visits home. In
her teens, Hui Ying Hung began dancing in
the street to make some extra money, and in

1976 she was spotted by Shaw Brothers maestro (and Hung Kuen god) Liu Chia Liang, who convinced her to join Shaws as a trainee actress.

Training complete, Miss Hui was signed to king director Chang Cheh's camp, with her first role coming in Fu Sheng's classic *Chinatown Kid* (1977). She went on to appear in a further four Fu Sheng films: *Brave Archer* 1 and 2 (1977, 1978), *Life Gamble* (1977) for Chang Cheh, and Sun Chong's classic *Deadly Breaking Sword* (1979). She also appeared in *Invincible Shaolin* (1978).

From here Hui Ying Hung's career went into overdrive, when she was assigned to Liu Chia Liang's camp for the classic *Dirty Ho* (1979). Her remarkable physical ability so impressed Liu Sifu that he took her under his Hung Kuen wing. He cast her as his sister in the epic vengeance film *Mad Monkey Kung Fu*, where she let loose some fine kung fu against villain Lo Lieh. A co-starring role in the awesome *Fist/Clan of the White Lotus* (1980) followed, where she demonstrated some incredibly intricate embroidery fist.

Following these came the film that gained Hui Ying Hung the crown as queen of kung fu. *My Young Auntie* (1980) was a classy production that showcased her skill to the max in some incredible martial arts battles.

Above:

Hui Ying Hung poses for the camera

Right:

The Brave Archer

Rosa

My Young Auntie

The role won her the best actress award at the Asian Film Festival. Auntie, as she became known, then took centre stage in *Tigress of Shaolin* alongside Liu Chia Liang's sister and his nephew Liu Chia Yong. This was a slightly odd, but highly enjoyable tale of love, life and leprosy fist.

1981 saw Auntie alongside Liu Chia Hui in Liu Chia Liang's epic Wong Fei Hung tale *Martial Club.* Then production began on *Eight Diagram Pole Fighter,* with Hui Ying Hung taking a small role behind Fu Sheng and Liu Chia Hui, who headed the movie. The film went onto the back burner when Fu Sheng broke both his legs during production, and sadly wasn't completed until after his death in July 1983.

Auntie and the Liu clan gathered for *Legendary Weapons of Kung Fu* (1982). Then

Hui Ying Hung faces off against Meng Yuan Man in Lover's Blades

came a small non-fighting role as Adam Cheng's sister in the classic *Cat vs Rat* (1982). Liu Chia Liang then gave Auntie centre stage

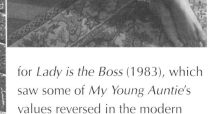

Two of her more recent stunning glamour poses, demonstrating another side to Hui Ying Hung, which is sadly yet to be seen on the big screen

not the most action packed film of all time, it contained a tremendous finalé with both Yuen and Auntie in fine form. Following this she appeared in *Inspector Wears A Skirt* part 1, alongside Cynthia Rothrock, Sibelle Hu and a whole host of comedy stars. Though the film has its highlights, it's a very slight piece of entertainment. Auntie also took a starring role in the less than brilliant sequel in 1988.

Hui Ying Hung starred in a whole host of femme fatale actioners towards the close of the eighties, from *Bad Boys Inc.* to *They Came to Rob Hong Kong*. She also appeared in several movies with Japanese action goddess Yukari Oshima – *Brave Young Girls*, *Never Say Regret*, Frankie Chan's dark masterpiece *Burning Ambition* and *That's Money*. She toplined the Hong Kong movie version of Linda La Plante's *Widows*, entitled *Widow Warriors*, which saw her appearing with actress Tien Niu for the first time since *Brave Archer*.

Taiwanese directorial maniac Robert Tai sought out Hui Ying Hung's services for his *Legend of the Drunken Tiger* (1990). Under Tai's choreographic madness, Auntie shows her traditional kung fu skills are still sharp.

1991 saw Hui Ying Hung in the Peking Opera drama *Stage Door Johnny*, which, like the *Inspector Wears A Skirt* movies, was produced by Jackie Chan. She then appeared in the extremely underrated and very violent *Roar of the Vietnamese* (1992), as a Vietnamese refugee forced into committing crime for a heartless Waise Lee.

With the coming of the new wave of 'traditional' kung fu films, kicked off by Jet Lee's epic *Once Upon A Time in China*, Hu

for *Lady is the Boss* (1983), which saw some of *My Young Auntie*'s values reversed in the modern world.

After completing *Eight Diagram Pole Fighter* in 1984, Hui Ying Hung left Liu Chia Liang's camp and went on to star in swordplay movies for many directors until Shaw Brothers ceased production in 1985.

Auntie next turned up in a seriously unfunny comedy scene in Samo Hung's *Twinkle Twinkle Lucky Stars* (1985). She then starred alongside Yuen Biao in *Rosa* (1985). While it's

Hui Ying Hung – the picture of innocence in Legendary Weapons of Kung Fu

Lover's Blades

Ying Hung appeared in a ghastly attempted remake of King Hu's *A Touch of Zen* called *Zen of Sword* (1993).

Auntie then gave her time to the fourth instalment of the *Inspector Wears A Skirt* series, starring Moon Lee and Cynthia Khan, the star of *Zen of Sword*. Auntie recreated her character from the first two parts as this rather tiresome series reached its conclusion.

Since 1994 and the TV movie *Kung Fu Mistress*, Auntie's activities have been covered by a shroud of mystery. To claim her career is over is to overlook the fact that she has lasted through all the changing genres of Hong Kong cinema and is the only one of her generation to still be working in the nineties. Although she never appears as the vamp on screen, recent photographs show that beneath that Mandarin fighting robe lie the qualities of a true Asian babe who could easily be cast in

Hui Ying Hung rides into town in the 1990 production *Legend of the Drunken Tiger*

more dramatic and erotic roles. When one considers the nature of Hong Kong's star-driven cinema industry, Hui Ying Hung's career is one hell of an achievement.

AUNTIE-ography Hui Ying Hung

惠英紅

1977	The Chinatown Kid	1985	The Inspector Wears a Skirt	
	The Brave Archer		Return of Pom Pom	
1978	The Brave Archer 2	1986	My Lucky Stars	
	Invincible Shaolin	1988	Mission Kill	
	Clan of Amazons		The Inspector Wears a Skirt 2	
1979	Deadly Breaking Sword		Dragon Family	
	Dirty Ho	1989	Burning Ambition	
	Mad Monkey Kung Fu		Widow Warriors	
1980	My Young Auntie		Bad Boys Inc.	
	Fist/Clan of the White Lotus		They Came to Rob Hong Kong	
	Tigress of Shaolin	198?	Do Unto Others	
	Lover's Blades	1990	Brave Young Girls	
	The Tiger and the Widow		Megaforce From the Highlands	
	Return to the 36th Chamber		Legend of the Drunken Tiger	
1981	The Martial Club		Never Say Regret	
	Return of the Sentimental Swordsman	1991	That's Money	
1982	Legendary Weapons of Kung Fu		Visa To Hell	
	Cat Versus Rat		Stage Door Johnny	
	Story of Sun Yat Sun	1992	Queen of Gamble	
1983	Lady is the Boss		On Parole	
	Buddhist Palm		Roar of the Vietnamese	
1984	Long Road to Gallantry	1993	Zen of Sword	
	Eight Diagram Pole Fighter		Madam City Hunter	
	New Tales of the Flying Fox		Vengeance of Six Dragons	
	Pool of Blood		The Inspector Wears a Skirt 4	
1985	Twinkle Twinkle Lucky Stars	1994	Kung Fu Mistress (TV)	
	Rosa	1996	Dragon From Shaolin	

MOON LEE
李賽鳳

YUKARI OSHIMA
大島由加利

blood sisters

Moon Lee versus The Osh in Avenging Quartet

moon lee & yukari oshima

text:
Rick Baker

Moon Lee and Yukari Oshima are ready and willing in a publicity shot from Dreaming the Reality

The Osh and Moon Lee do battle in Beauty Investigators

It **was in the** mid to late eighties that a new band of modern day heroines began to make ripples in the UK. They could be regarded as the four femmes – and Michelle Yeoh (or Michelle Khan as she was then known) and Cynthia Khan (no relation) were two of that pack of vixens who were starting to catch the eye of the male western movie entrepreneur. But in the following pages we will focus our attention on the other half of this avenging quartet: Moon Lee (or Mona Lee as she's known in some European countries) and Yukari Oshima (also known as Cynthia Luster).

This pair were simultaneously launched in the groundbreaking femme fatale action flick *Angel* (1988), one of the first films of this genre to find its way onto UK video shelves. It was released by CBS Fox as *Iron Angels*, the title having been changed by German film distributor Atlas, who were representing it in Europe and wanted to give it greater impact. Atlas were also responsible for representing Hong Kong movies like the *Mad Mission* films (*Aces Go Places*) and John Woo's *A Better Tomorrow* (1986).

However, *Angel* already had a history in the UK prior to its video release, as there was a thriving Chinese film circuit around the country, playing in most of the major cities. At this time I had a stall in Gerard Street in London's Chinatown selling badges and sunglasses, right next to where they used to put posters advertising future Hong Kong movie releases screening in Leicester Square. I distinctly remember the *Angel* poster getting a lot of attention, not due to the two starring ladies but because of two other names listed on the credits, veteran Shaw Brothers actor David Chiang and awesome kicker Hwang Jan Lee, who had become legendary amongst the regular cinema goers in the seventies and early eighties. It wasn't that we understood the Chinese characters, but their faces, predominant on the poster, had to lend the movie a certain credibility. By no means was *Angel* either Yukari Oshima or Moon Lee's first taste of acting, but it was certainly this film that projected both into the western eye, and their following steadily grew going into the nineties. Over the next few pages we'll take a more in depth look at two of the UK's most popular femme fatale action stars, who have become blood sisters.

MOON LEE

Moon Lee (Lee Choi Fong) was born in Hong Kong on February 14, 1965. She joined the RTV studios after finishing her secondary education and made her screen debut in a TV programme called *Affection on Earth*. During the early eighties she was to appear in a dozen or so TV series, and it was during this period that she played her first movie role, under the watchful eye of Tsui Hark, in the cult movie *Zu: Warriors From the Magic Mountain* (1983). Her part, although only a co-starring role alongside such screen greats as Yuen Biao, Meng Hoi and super screen starlet Brigitte Lin, was predominant enough to make an impression, and she was to team up with Yuen Biao for a second time that year in the kung fu football flick *The Champions*. She then returned to TV roles, although in Hong Kong this is no bad thing as soap stars are as admired and as much in the public's eye as movie stars. One of these roles was as the fighting star of a kung fu series called *Drunken Fist Boxer*.

In 1985, Jackie Chan teamed up with James Glickenhaus to shoot *The Protector* for Warner Brothers. It was shot on location in

Moon with the deadly
nunchakus – Angel

Oshima, was to revitalise the whole genre of Hong Kong bad girl cinema. The word 'Angel' was subsequently used in countless other movies like *Angel Terminator*, *Revenge of Angel* and *Angel Enforcers*, and came to imply femme fatale action at its most feisty.

In the winter of 1994, while shooting interviews for the *Eastern Heroes Video Magazine*, we were looking to put together a femme fatale section and were fortunate enough to discover that our obvious choice, Moon Lee, was in Hong Kong at the time. She agreed to meet us at the offices of

Hong Kong and America, and so casting had to take place on both sides of the globe. Moon was cast as Soo Ling, the cute daughter of one of Jackie's contacts. Despite her limited dialogue which was obviously dubbed, her role was far more than a cameo, and she is one of the few Hong Kong actresses who can not only say that she's starred alongside Jackie Chan, but also that she's been in an international film. However, the film wasn't particularly successful, and following it she continued working in Hong Kong TV.

In 1985 Moon Lee co-starred alongside Lam Ching Ying in *Mr Vampire*, which proved a huge success in Hong Kong, and in 1986 she returned to the big screen, once again starring alongside Yuen Biao, her movie big brother, in *Mr Vampire 2*, although at this stage her big screen persona as a fighter had still not developed and she was cast as a hapless girl-next-door character. But things were about to change when in 1988 she was cast as the main lead in *Angel*, which was to transform her career dramatically. This movie, in which Moon Lee starred with Yukari

director/actor Tsui Siu Ming, which was a double bonus for us as he is a key figure in Hong Kong movies.

As Moon bounced through the door we could instantly see that she was as cute and pretty as her screen image. With long, glossy black hair and a girlish face she is

Right:

Moon Lee in her

movie debut Zu:

Warriors From the

Magic Mountain,

alongside Yuen

Biao and Meng Hoi

Above:

Moon Lee

poses for the

cameras

Moon Lee in Mr Vampire 2, in the days when

her fighting persona was yet to be developed

personable in a sweet, girl-next-door way, rather than a screen vamp. Her tiny figure was dwarfed by myself and my partner Toby, both rather strapping fellows, and at first glance she was probably glad she'd agreed to meet us in a busy office rather than someplace else! Sadly Moon's English isn't good enough for her to be able to express herself fluently, but as Toby speaks Cantonese we were able to chat freely, and anyone who's seen the video magazine will know how vivacious and spirited her conversation was.

I asked Moon if she'd started learning kung fu for her role in *Angel*, or

Moon Lee

demonstrates

her ballet

training

Moon Lee. Angelic looks but a lethal bundle of fury

Moon Lee in full military regalia in Angel 2

The babe gets tough – Dreaming the Reality

whether she'd studied it earlier in her career. She explained that she'd begun to learn as soon as she became an actress, and that her mentor was Tsui Siu Ming. She didn't find it that difficult to adapt because she trained from an early age in ballet and classical dancing, and she'd found this very helpful when it came to learning martial arts.

"People often ask me if I have learnt kung fu from an early age, because I seem so competent, and they are surprised when I tell them no," she said.

We asked if her tough girl image put men off, because she seemed so agressive on screen. "I have to give one hundred percent on screen, but in reality I'm a very sweet girl who doesn't like fighting at all! *Angel* is a film which I really like. This is the film which made me a star and established me as an action actress. I really put a lot of effort into making it. Although not the best of films in terms of production value, I still regard this as a special film for me." Was it tough making a film like *Angel*? "It's very hard. You have to

Beauty Investigators

Moon Lee versus Yuen Wah in Bury Me High

Moon Lee in a more sultry pose

be very brave and take many risks, because in this industry if you're injured or even killed nobody cares and there are plenty of people out there ready to take your place. I have had many narrow escapes in my career. I won't do any dangerous stunts unless I've thought about it first."

How does she psyche herself up for a role? "I never think, 'oh I'm a girl, I shouldn't be doing that'. I just think of myself as a man, because if I don't, I won't appear powerful on screen."

You've made quite a few films with Yukari Oshima – do you like working with her? "Yes, she is a very good female action star and she is lots of fun on set, but like me she would like to do more serious drama roles. I would really like to play the role of a poor and gentle girl who can make the audience cry, but I've had no chance yet."

Above:
On both sides
of the gun.
Condor
Mission

The next Gong Li, perhaps? "She is a wonderful actress. I don't know if I could be that good but I would like the opportunity to try."

Did Moon find herself, after the success of *Angel*, being inundated with action scripts? "Yes, I had many offers, but actually before I made *Angel 2*, I returned to do another movie, which was a drama without any fighting, called *Midnight Whispers*. But since then, I am always cast in the action role."

Moon Lee's success in *Angel* spawned two sequels (1988, 1989). It was during the filming of *Angel 3* that she demonstrated the true extent of her martial arts skill by fighting

Moon Lee proves that even with roller skates she can still kick ass – Nocturnal Demon

Above: Action Moon Lee style – New Kids in Town

Left: Angel 4 poster art, prominently featuring Moon Lee

off more than a dozen men with a pair of nunchakus, a weapon which is seldom associated with female fighters and which would certainly not make it past the censors if the film were to be released in the UK. It's a scene that's one of my personal favourite moments out of all her movies, and gave her an edge over other actresses of the same calibre who probably wouldn't have the skill required to contemplate doing such a scene.

Despite Moon Lee's talent, her Hong Kong box office pull has not been so notable, unlike in the Philippines, (the same is true of Yukari Oshima). This may be why during my meeting with Moon Lee she told me that she had decided to hang up her kung fu pumps and had set up her own school to teach ballet, her first love. She was quite taken aback when I told her how popular she is in the west. She is one of the actresses I received the most enquiries about in the early nineties, which was quite staggering considering only two of her movies were available on video in the UK – *Iron Angels* (*Angel*) and *The Protector*, although I doubt most people would even know she was in that. However, in the past year the general rise of the Hong Kong scene in the west has made a healthy range of her movies available and brought her back into the public eye.

Although it is unlikely that we will be blessed with all of her films in the UK, more

left: Moon Lee practices with 'The Pops', Liu Chia Liang, in New Kids in Town

and more of them are finding their way onto the video shelf, many of them on the Eastern Heroes label. One that I doubt will turn up, but which is interesting to see, is the 1992 film *A Serious Shock: Yes Madam 2*, in which Moon actually plays a villainess for the first time, coming fist to fingernail against Yukari Oshima and Cynthia Khan. In Hong Kong, where I first purchased this film, I was surprised to see it was rated Category III. I raced back to watch it, hoping it would contain nudity scenes of Ms Lee and Ms Oshima, but no such luck. The rating is probably attributable to the violent scenes, in one of which Moon beats a young cop almost to death during a judo class, showing that hell hath no fury like Moon Lee scorned. Her

Lee. It is worth noting that the title has since been changed for the international market to *Death Triangle*.

Other films that feature notable performances from Moon Lee are *Princess Madam* (1989), *Killer Angels* (1989), *New Kids in Town* (1989), *Fatal Termination* (1989), *Bury Me High* (directed by and starring her kung fu sifu Tsui Siu Ming, 1991) and *Dreaming the Reality* (1991), which saw her rekindle the chemistry with Yukari Oshima. One of her most disappointing films is *Avenging Quartet* (1993). The glossy sleeve depicts Moon, Michiko, Yukari Oshima and Cynthia Khan as leather clad women on motorcycles, but unfortunately the movie does not live up to the sleeve's sexy image. Still, it's a great buy if you just want a good shot of Moon Lee!

When I spoke to Moon in 1994 she said she was tired of making low budget femme fatale flicks and that was why she had decided to go into semi-retirement until she was offered more demanding roles. Since then, I'm happy to say that she has signed up with TVB to make a kung fu series called *Northern Leg Southern Fist* (literal English translation) alongside the star of *Story of Riki*, Fan Siu Wong. The series has been very successful on Hong Kong TV and a second series has been put into production. Moon plays the northern leg, and from the glimpses I've seen of it, I have to say her kung fu skills are back on top form. Let's hope this inspires her to return to the big screen once again. Even though she gets little critical acclaim in Hong Kong for her movie roles, there would be a lot of disappointed fans in the west if she decided to quit the movie scene for good.

Champions

Moon Lee with Fan Siu Wong in a publicity shot for TVB's Northern Leg, Southern Fist TV series

Revenge of Angel

wrath continues throughout the film as she mercilessly tortures anyone who gets in her way. One guy gets skewered straight through the mouth with a barbecue fork. At the climax we see Cynthia Khan and Yukari Oshima unleash their skills to finally defeat the psychotic Moon

Like all good girls, Moon doesn't take kindly to having her handbag snatched! New Kids in Town

MOON-ography 李賽鳳

Moon Lee / Lee Choi Fong

1983	Zu: Warriors From the Magic Mountain
1984	Golden Queen's Commandos
1983	Champions
1985	Mr Vampire
	The Protector
1986	Mr Vampire 2
1988	Angel aka Iron Angels
	Midnight Whispers
	Angel 2
1989	Princess Madam
	Killer Angels
	Fatal Termination
	New Kids in Town aka New Killers in Town
	Angel 3
1990	Revenge of Angel
1991	Dreaming the Reality
	Bury Me High
	Nocturnal Demon
	Angel Force
	Mission of Condor
1992	Beauty Investigator
	A Serious Shock: Yes Madam 2 aka Death Triangle
	Kickboxer's Tears
	Mission of Justice
	The Big Deal
	Angel Project
1993	Avenging Quartet
	The Inspector Wears a Skirt 4
	Angel Terminator 2
	Angel 4
1994	Little Heroes
1996	Northern Leg Southern Fist (TV series)

大島由加利 OSH-ography
Yukari Oshima / Cynthia Luster / Dai Do / Yukari Tsumara

1986	Kung Fu Wonderchild	1992	Hard to Kill
1987	Shanghai Express		Mission of Justice
	Funny Family		Beauty Investigator
1988	Angel		Fatal Chase
1989	A Book of Heroes		Death Triangle
	Burning Ambition		Story of Riki
	Godfather's Daughter Mafia Blues		Kickboxer's Tears
	Angels Mission		Angel of Vengeance
	Framed		The Big Deal
	Final Run aka Kick Fighters		Devil Girl 18 (cameo)
	A Punch to Revenge	1993	Ultra Cop 2000
1990	Brave Young Girls		Avenging Quartet
	Outlaw Brothers		Project S
	Close Escape		Angel Terminators 2
	Never Say Regret		The Cat aka Cat's Claw Kung Fu
	That's Money		Lethal Panther 2
	Lucky Seven 2		Honour and Glory
1991	Dreaming the Reality		aka Angel the Kickboxer
	Story of the Gun	1994	Guardian Angel
	Midnight Angel		To Live and Die in Manila
	Angel Terminator 2	1995	Direct Line
	Angel Hunter		Deadly Target
	Ghost Love		The Drugs Fighters
	Spiritually a Cop	199?	His Way, Her Way, Their Ways
		?	Angel Force

YUKARI OSHIMA

Born in Fukuoka, Japan, Yukari Oshima is known by various names depending upon what part of the world you live in. In parts of Europe she goes by the terrifically marketable moniker Cynthia Luster; In Hong Kong she's known as Dai Do; on some press books her name is reversed, Chinese style, as Oshima Yukari; she's also been credited as Yukari Tsumara; but in England we simply refer to her as 'the Osh'. Here in the UK she is credited on all video sleeves as Yukari Oshima, except for those put out by Imperial Entertainment, who prefer her European name Cynthia Luster.

As a young girl, Yukari was a kung fu fanatic. Her idols were Sue Shiomi, star of *Sister Streetfighter*, Yuen Biao and Sylvester Stallone. Her first interest in films was sparked by watching Japanese chanbara swordplay movies. At the age of 13 she started to study gogu ryu karate under the watchful eye of karate master Miki and it is rumoured she won a national kata championship at the age of 16. She also learnt gymnastics and judo at school.

Prior to her first break onto the Japanese television screen, Yukari studied for a year with Sonny Chiba, learning to do stunts. Her early work on Japanese TV included episodes of *Dynaman* and *Space Sheriff Gavan*, although here she was unrecognisable as her costume covered her completely. She also played the villainous henchwoman Fara Cat in *Shodenshi Bioman*.

Despite her break into Japanese TV, she was still convinced that Hong Kong action films were superior to homegrown flicks, and her big opportunity came in 1987. Yasuaki Kurata, an associate of her martial arts master and martial arts movie star, had

landed a role in the movie *Shanghai Express* (aka *Millionaires Express*) and he invited her to screen test for a role. This was to be a dream come true for her. Not only was the role to be a Japanese Samurai woman – a character from one of her favourite movie genres – but she was to act alongside her screen favourite Yuen Biao, with her martial arts skills tuned up by director Samo Hung.

Shanghai Express, which has become a cult film for western followers, was a superb showcase for the Osh.

Publicity shot for Godfather's Daughter Mafia Blues

Right: The Osh and Dick Wei in Final Run

Don't...

...get...

...me...

...mad!

Despite only playing a small supporting role, her presence makes a considerable impact. The cast includes everyone who's anyone in Hong Kong cinema, including Cynthia Rothrock who was the flavour of the moment among female stars, but Oshima is certainly not overshadowed.

With a successful Hong Kong film under her belt, Yukari relocated to Taiwan and started to find work with little trouble. Her first film there was *Funny Family* (1987) for director Chu Yen Ping, followed by *A Book of Heroes* (1989) for the same director. In the UK, the madcap action comedy *A Book of*

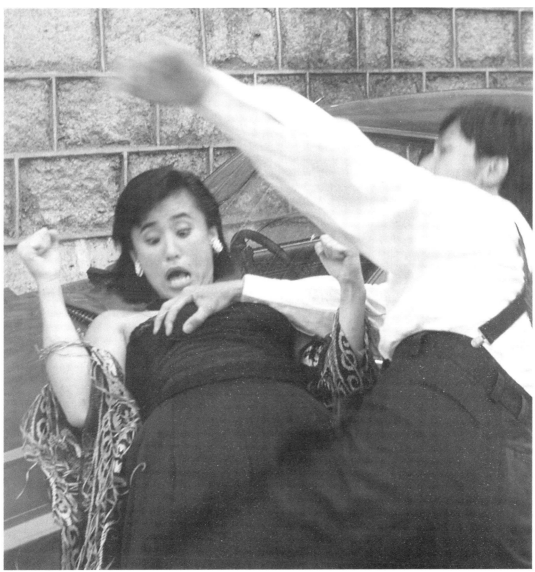

Heroes is far better known as it played the Chinese cinema circuit, and *Funny Family* is usually known as *A Book of Heroes 2*, although it actually preceded it.

Although Yukari found Taiwanese film production somewhat slower paced than Hong Kong, *A Book of Heroes* was another excellent showcase for her skills. Unlike many other female stars emerging at this time, she had a genuine martial arts background which gave her a distinct advantage on screen, and her prowess began to catch the viewing public's eye.

In 1988 Yukari made the thriller *Angel*, which was to establish her as a big star in Europe. Of all her Taiwanese movies it is the one which most resembles a Hong Kong film, and as reported in previous pages, it was here that she first stood her ground against Moon Lee. *Angel* was to be a huge success, and unlike her previous Taiwanese films where she was more or less cast as a jewel in the garbage, the box office success promoted her

Angel the Kickboxer publicity artwork

Dreaming the Reality

to star status. Unfortunately, critics have given neither Yukari nor Moon Lee the respect that both artists warrant. Compared to stars like Cynthia Rothrock and Michelle Yeoh, their press coverage was virtually nonexistent in Hong Kong. However, any star who proves bankable in Taiwan, the Philippines or Thailand is guaranteed plenty more work, and the offers came flooding in.

In 1989 director Frankie Chan cast Yukari in the

Deadly Target poster artwork, featuring Yeung Pan Pan

Above and below:
Face of an angel, eyes
of a killer. The Osh in
fighting mood

riproaring action flick *Burning Ambition*, in which he also starred along with up and coming heart-throb Simon Yam. After several more features she returned to Hong Kong to star in what I consider to be her best film, *Outlaw Brothers* (1990), which once again starred and was directed by Frankie Chan. Here she plays a policewoman hot on the tail of a notorious thief of exotic cars.

On the set she met up with British born action star Mark Houghton, whom she'd previously encountered while filming *Final*

Mean and moody in Guardian Angel

Run (aka *Kick Fighters*). *Final Run* was also a great showcase for her fighting skills, if only for the final reel. Mark taught Yukari Hung Gar for a while, and said: "During the period that I trained her, despite her martial art background she didn't seem to know an awful lot. In fact I suspect she had just learnt what she needed to know to make action movies." If this was true, the short period she spent training with Mark paid dividends for *Outlaw Brothers*. Her confidence as a fighting star had increased tenfold and in deference to Mark she used the famous Hung Kuen one finger raised en garde stance.

Another Japanese star, Michiko Nishiwaki, also appeared in *Outlaw Brothers*. However,

Road rage Oshima style – Lethal Panther 2

The Osh practices her stances…

Block that… Never Say Regret

She's bootiful! Oshima pairs off against Yeung Pan Pan in Deadly Target

while Michiko was pretty much just window dressing, the Osh, with brawn as well as beauty, reigned supreme. *Outlaw Brothers* has never been released in Britain, but it's highly recommended that you see it if you get the chance, to appreciate the full blown talent of Yukari Oshima. She dominates three major fight scenes, demolishing a roomful of bad guys in a hot car shop, taking out tough guys in glorious slo-mo in a poolside fracas, and finally out-Brucing Lee in a showdown with American martial artist Jeff Falcon.

Vincent Lyn, another American martial artist who had a small part in the movie, told me during a visit to the UK that she was a really tough cookie. There was one point where he was supposed to kick her arms: "No matter how much I tried, I kept missing and kicking her in the chest. Despite this she never complained once. I found her totally great although after the shot, not surprisingly, I did get some grief from Frankie Chan."

After such strong performances in *Angel* and *Outlaw Brothers*, Yukari's feisty femme

Dreaming the Reality

fatale persona began to reward her with a constant stream of work between Hong Kong and Taiwan. She was never quite to recapture the quality roles of this period, but her fame was now bringing her international recognition among Hong Kong movie fans. She has never found the mainstream success of Maggie Cheung or Michelle Yeoh, but instead became queen of the B movies whose high action quota endeared her to European fans.

One enjoyable oddity that Yukari starred in was *Kung Fu Wonderchild* (1986), a Taiwanese flick in which she appears alongside Taiwanese babe Lin Shao Lou, known in the west as Sharon Foster. *Kung Fu*

Story of the Gun

Ultra Cop 2000

In Yukari's case, two guns are better than one! Brave Young Girls

Wonderchild is a bizarre *Zu: Warriors* style movie incorporating some animation, but despite its fantasy element it allowed the Osh to strut her stuff to an impressive standard.

Gradually Yukari's roles were becoming more varied, allowing her to play the heroine as well as the aggressor. Throughout 1991 she put in memorable appearances in movies like *Midnight Angel*, *Story of the Gun* and *Dreaming the Reality*, which reunited her with Moon Lee. Here they played glamorous sisters trained by their father since childhood to be assassins. Yukari is pitched once again as the more aggressive of the two, and they are joined by a third feisty femme fatale, Sibelle Hu.

The following year Yukari returned to shoot a film for Golden Harvest, who had given her the first big break in *Shanghai Express*. *Story of Riki* was to become a cult film among fans of the more gory side of Hong Kong cinema, although sadly it made little impact in Hong Kong itself. The film, a Manga-in-Motion style adaptation of *King of Power*, starring Fan Siu Wong, has Yukari playing the unusual role of a transsexual convict who has been awarded the position of trustee to help keep the other inmates under control. The film is notable for its comic book violence, which never stints on the blood and guts, rather than for Yukari's presence.

Yukari continued to churn out films which made little impact on the Hong Kong box office – in fact, some of them went straight to video – but retained her popularity in Taiwan and the Philippines. In 1992 her pairings with Moon Lee became more frequent, and they starred together in *Kickboxer's Tears*, *Beauty Investigator* and *Avenging Quartet* (1993). Despite having two such formidable action actresses sharing the screen, these are actually some of the weaker movies of their careers.

In 1993 Yukari had a small cameo role alongside Cynthia Rothrock in *Angel the Kickboxer*, directed by Godfrey Ho, who also directed the femme fatale action movie *Lethal Panther* (released in the UK as *Deadly China Dolls*). Yukari's scene was cut for the British release, which was retitled *Honour and Glory*, so Osh fans should seek out the Hong Kong version. In the same year she landed a part in the Golden Harvest film *Project S*, which starred Asian beauty Michelle Yeoh.

Above:
The Osh in Japanese mode – Avenging Quartet

Right:
Yukari gets to grips with the enemy – Beauty Investigators

出品人⋯⋯吳明才
監製⋯⋯張賓榮才
導演⋯⋯李賓鳳
李賓鳳
主演⋯⋯大島田加里
金志姬
制片⋯⋯黃比利
編劇⋯⋯曾正義
導演⋯⋯

Beauty Investigator

Above:
Yukari and Robin Shou
in Hard to Kill
Top left:
Publicity artwork for Beauty
Investigator, featuring Yukari
Oshima and Moon Lee

Left:
Yukari kicks high in
Outlaw Brothers

interviewing Yukari for his successful documentary *Cinema of Vengeance* (1995).

It was once hoped that Yukari would make a visit to the UK. She was invited some years ago to be the guest of honour at the Clash of the Titans martial arts event held in the Midlands. Sadly, due to work commitments she was unable to come, and was replaced by *No Retreat No Surrender* star Loren Avedon. I believe Yukari is totally unaware of her cult status in the west. But who knows, in the future we may persuade her to come and bask in the admiration of her western fans.

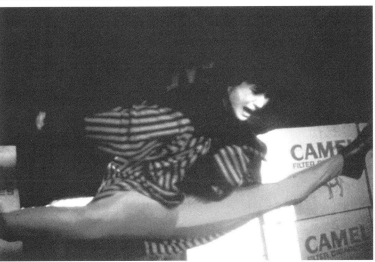

Despite his blink-or-you'll-miss-it role, Yukari could now proudly announce that she'd appeared in a film with Jackie Chan!

Her near misses with Golden Harvest notwithstanding, it seems that Yukari's film heyday has passed by and it is unlikely she'll ever get the recognition or cult status in Hong Kong that she has achieved in the west. In the last couple of years she has married and divorced martial art actor Mark Cheng, with whom she had a superb screen fight in the above average *Hard to Kill*, also starring Robin Shou. She has continued to fight fist to fingernail in low budget Philippino produced movies, including *Guardian Angel* (1994), *Deadly Target* and *Angel Force*, which coincidentally has my partner and co-author of this book, Toby Russell, playing a white slave trader. Toby also had the pleasure of

Despite starring in several Category III movies, the Osh has yet to reveal any of her assets on the big screen, although there is a rumour that she has posed for the tame Hong Kong edition of *Playboy* or *Penthouse*. I've never unearthed this on any of my trips to Hong Kong, so I'm unable to confirm or deny the rumour, but if anyone out there actually possesses it, send it in to Eastern Heroes so we can settle the matter once and for all. Until then, I'll treat it like Mulder and Scully, as an X-File: case unsolved...

Yukari Oshima kicks out in
Brave Young Girls

MAGGIE CHEUNG
ANITA MUI
MICHELLE YEOH

梅艷芳　　楊紫瓊　　張曼玉

the heroic trio

maggie cheung, anita mui, michelle yeoh

text: **Rick Baker**

Maggie

Anita!

Michelle!

This bevy of Chinese beauties has only come to the attention of western audiences in the nineties, mainly because all three are top-drawer performers who star in high budget movies, and acquiring these movies for release is somewhat more expensive than those of the killer B femme fatale stars.

All three actresses established their careers in the eighties, but the rise in the popularity of Hong Kong movies in the west during the nineties has allowed these three deadly China dolls to come to the forefront. Previously, only the hardcore movie fans of the mid to late eighties would have been able to identify

Two's company – three's a fantasy

these stars of the Jade Screen, but when all three were cast together in the atmospheric and memorable *The Heroic Trio* (1993), they began to shine like the true stars they were. Of course, we admired them for their acting skill – but the downright sexy outfits did go a long way when it came to catching the eye of the redblooded western male.

Sadly, living in the UK, we don't have the multitude of Chinatown video shops that our friends in the United States do, and with the heavy levy of UK censorship and the high price of these classy movies, there aren't

so many opportunities to see them. So in the UK we may be late starters, but already the three ladies in question have acquired a legion of fans and are likely to remain in the public eye well into the next century. Having seen them magically cast together in *The Heroic Trio* and its sequel, *Executioners* (1993) it is only to be hoped that stars of such magnitude can be united on screen again.

Of course, having captured your attention with *The Heroic Trio*, the smart fan will want to check out the movies of each actress individually. It's a little like the case of Jackie Chan, Samo Hung and Yuen Biao, another classic trio: when they parted ways after *Dragons Forever* in 1987, interest in the film career of each grew apace.

The presence of Maggie, Anita and Michelle in Hong Kong cinema hasn't just captivated a male audience, though. Their

Come and have a go if you think you're hard enough

'Thelma and Louise' kick-ass attitude has won them plenty of female fans too. Men want them, women want to be them, and the reason? Because they're so cool...

MAGGIE CHEUNG

張曼玉

Born in Hong Kong on September 20, 1964, Maggie emigrated to England when she was eight, returning to Hong Kong after completing her education. Starting out as a model, she was runner up in the Miss Hong Kong contest, which made her immediately famous; Wong Jing cast her in a Cherrie Chung comedy, *Prince Charming*, only a week after the pageant.

"After that and a film with director Taylor Wong, I did TV work for two years because it was part of the contract for Miss Hong Kong," Maggie told me when I interviewed her in 1994. "It was a nightmare! I hated it and I was lucky to be busy in film work too so I didn't have to go back. After that I signed up to Shaw Brothers for six films but shortly after that they stopped a lot of productions, so after all these years I still owe them one picture!"

During this period, Maggie appeared in many low budget comedies and television series, mainly cast as the girl-next-door type. "It took about four years before I got sick of doing the same kind of role," she explained. "I grew up. When you're 23, you're very different to when you're 18. I felt I'd matured a lot and I couldn't always be the girl-next-

Moon Warriors
photo showcase

door or the stupid little girl that they kicked down the stairs. I wanted to change the parts I was doing, but it wasn't until *As Tears Go By* came along that my career changed direction. I like having the balance of both worlds; at one time, around the time of *Farewell, China*, I was doing a bunch of serious heavy drama movies, and the audience let me know that they wanted to see me in comedies as well. I felt myself that it had become a kind of habit to work on those movies, I'd lost the sparkle."

Indeed, it was two very different roles that helped to make Maggie the big star she is today. The first was the role of Jackie Chan's girlfriend May in *Police Story* (1985), in which she was the cute, wholesome sidekick in a lighthearted action flick; the other was in Wong Kar Wai's powerful arthouse movie *As Tears Go By* (1988), which revealed her breadth as an actress, won much critical acclaim, and led to her being offered far more challenging roles. She won more acclaim for her performance in Stanley Kwan's *Actress* (1992), for which she also won many prestigious international awards, including the Berlin Silver Bear.

"I'm very proud to have that and I don't usually speak too much about it for the sake of modesty, I don't want to get too bigheaded

Far left: A rare early shot of Maggie Cheung

Left: Maggie in beauty pageant mode

Maggie Cheung and Jacky Cheung (no relation!) claw out in Flying Daggers

Oh the indignity! Maggie Cheung gets messy in Paper Marriage

Left:
Police Story
playing the
estranged
girlfriend of
Jackie Chan

Middle left:
Ice Man
Cometh

Below:
Two Jackies
are better
than one?
Maggie has
an identity
crisis in Twin
Dragons

over it!" she revealed. "But it's something I have that nobody can take away from me. Before *As Tears Go By*, nobody thought I could do serious acting. They typecast me as the stupid girl-next-door. The girls who are holding guns in the movies now, it doesn't mean they can't do serious acting too, it's just that the chance hasn't come for them."

Maggie's acting talent, coupled with her beauty and flair for comedy, has led to her being offered a far broader variety of roles than many Hong Kong actresses get to play, and she has been a very prolific performer, doing everything from horror, for example *The Seventh Curse* with Chow Yun Fat (1986) to Heroic Bloodshed in *The First Shot* (1993). Notably, she has worked with the golden trio of Jackie Chan, Samo Hung and Yuen Biao, all of whom are guaranteed to get an up and coming actress noticed. With Jackie, she followed up the hugely successful *Police Story* with two sequels – she was badly

Above:
Maggie
Cheung has a
serious word
with
Andy Lau in
As Tears
Go By

Below:
Green Snake

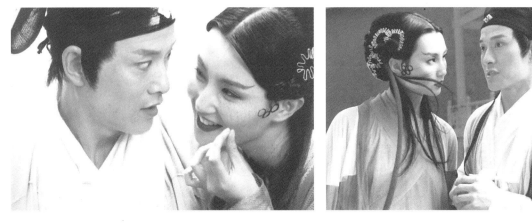

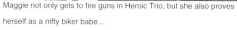
Maggie not only gets to fire guns in Heroic Trio, but she also proves herself as a nifty biker babe…

injured doing her own stunts in the second part – and also *Project A part 2* (1987) and *Twin Dragons* (1992). With Samo Hung, she made *Paper Marriage* (1988), playing a mud wrestling immigrant in a *Green Card* type situation, and with Yuen Biao she appeared as a happy hooker in *Iceman Cometh* aka *Time Warriors* (1988).

In fact, 1988 was a particularly busy year, with Maggie making a dozen or so films, and this rate of work was to continue into the nineties. As well as the more demanding arthouse roles she has excelled in new wave martial art style action. She's not really a screen fighter, or a fists and kicks girl, but she looks good in stylish new wave swordplay movies like *Dragon Gate Inn* and *Moon Warriors* (1992) and *Holy Weapon* aka *Seven Maidens* (1993), looking glamorous in flowing robes rather than taking part in hard physical combat.

However, the type of role she is most proud of is the arthouse movie. In 1990 she made *Red Dust*, which ironically replaced the world premiere of *Armour of God 2* at the

Above: The mean and moody innkeeper in Dragon Gate Inn

Right: Maggie and Ti Lung face off in First Shot

Slapstick in Holy Weapon

Moon Warriors

NFT here in London because Jackie's movie was behind schedule. Her second movie with Wong Kar Wai, *Days of Being Wild* (1990) was also critically acclaimed.

Up until 1993 Maggie was continuing to make movies at a great rate, including *The Heroic Trio* and its sequel, a very sexy performance alongside Joey Wong in Tsui Hark's erotic *Green Snake* and a romantic role in *The Barefoot Kid*. However, when I spoke to her in 1994 she had decided to cut down on her movie roles and concentrate on more special projects, perhaps influenced by the international success of Gong Li, whom she greatly admires: "My mind is set to do only the work that I really long to do. It doesn't matter if it doesn't come along, I just won't work," she told me. "I'm not going to work for money like I did before, or just for the sake of working. I'm quite happy to just relax and do things I look forward to doing and not rush myself. It's nice after all these years to have no plans."

Since then, after a break from the screen, Maggie's face has once again started to appear within the pages of Hong Kong magazines. She has completed the movie *The*

Sung Dynasty Family (1996) and is set to start work on a new drama with Stanley Kwan. She has already made well over seventy films, from comedy to arthouse to drama, and it will be interesting to see what lies ahead for one of Hong Kong's most popular, beautiful and talented leading ladies.

This page:
Maggie
Cheung in a
variety of
off-screen
poses

the essential guide to deadly china dolls • **85**

MAGGIE-ography
Maggie Cheung / Cheung Man Yuk

1984	Prince Charming
	Behind the Yellow Line
1985	Girl with the Diamond Slipper
	Police Story
	It's a Drink, it's a Bomb
1986	Rose
	Happy Ghost 3
	The Seventh Curse
1987	Sister Cupid
	Heartbeat 100
	The Romancing Star
	Project A part 2
1988	Girls Without Tomorrow
	Love Soldier Fortune
	Paper Marriage
	As Tears Go By
	Mother vs Mother
	Moon, Star, Sun
	How To Pick
	Police Story 2
	The Game They Call Sex
	The Nowhere Man
	Last Romance
	Ice Man Cometh aka Time Warriors
1989	The Bachelor's Swan Song
	Double Causes Troubles
	My Dear Son
	A Fishy Story
	Hearts No Flowers
	In Between Lovers
1990	Hearts into Hearts
	Full Moon in New York
	Song of Exile
	The Dragon From Russia
	Red Dust
	Farewell, China
	Days of Being Wild

1991	The Perfect Match
	Alan and Eric
	Will of Iron
	Today's Hero
1992	Final Justice
	Twin Dragons
	Actress
	What a Hero
	Police Story 3
	Dragon Gate Inn
	Rose
	True Love
	Moon Warriors
1993	Millionaire Cop
	The Heroic Trio
	The First Shot
	Too Happy For Words
	Holy Weapon aka Seven Maidens
	Flying Daggers
	The Enigma of Love
	The Mad Monk
	Boys Are Easy
	Green Snake
	Heroic Trio 2: Executioners
	The Barefoot Kid
	Two Eagles Shooting Heroes
1994	Ashes of Time
	In Between
1996	Sung Dynasty Family

張曼玉

A Fishy Story

Song of Exile

This page:

Maggie Cheung off screen

Left:

With Tony Leung on the set
of Flying Daggers

梅艷芳 ANITA MUI

Second of our trio of stars under the microscope is Anita Mui (Mui Yim Fong). In the UK she was probably the last of the heroic trio to be discovered. Awareness of her came not via video but courtesy of Channel Four. After the success of Jonathan Ross' *Incredibly Strange Film Show* he was invited to select a season of movies for Xmas 1989. One of the films he chose to be screened was *Rouge* (1987), and it was here that the UK audience was first exposed to the haunting beauty of Ms Mui. She wasn't to be seen on video here until a couple of years later, when Imperial Entertainment released *Mr Canton and Lady Rose* aka *Miracles* (1989). In this, although she had a co-starring role, she was overshadowed by Jackie Chan, whom most of the viewers would already have been familiar with. Despite this earlier lack of exposure, in recent years she has come to the forefront of Hong Kong movie fans' attention. Born on October 10, 1963 and raised in the Guangsi province of China, Anita was one of four children. Her father died when she was a child and she embarked upon a career in entertainment to do her bit as family breadwinner, singing and dancing while touring with her mother's cabaret. But it was some years before her musical ability was recognised.

In 1982, Anita won first place in a Hong Kong talent contest, often the way actors and

actresses can get on the first rung of the ladder to success. The show, largely sponsored by TVB, the biggest TV network in Hong Kong, was a frequent way of discovering new talent.

Anita started out singing many theme tunes for well-known movies. Her first major appearance was shortly before the clock struck midnight to bring in the new year of 1986, when she played a sold out concert at the Hong Kong Coliseum. She continued to sell out a staggering fifteen concerts in a row, and in doing so established herself as one of the first female singers to create a sensation in the male dominated Hong Kong music industry. She was to become the Madonna of Hong Kong pop, and one of her most popular songs, *Bad Girl*, was to draw much attention for its sexually suggestive lyrics. As Anita's career moved into the fast

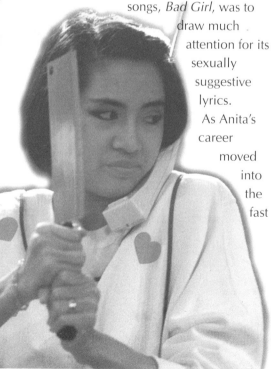

Follow the Star

"Anita Mui – stunning, sexy and very talented"

A sultry pose from

Fight Back To School 3

lane, her status moved towards megastardom. Her fame spread further afield thoughout Asia when she accepted the Special Asian Award bestowed upon her at the Tokyo Music Festival. Her first album, *Debt of the Heart*, was the first of an incredible seventeen albums to go platinum during the period 1985-1991. This allowed her the freedom to tour the world playing sell-out concerts, attracting hundreds of thousands of people. Her shows became famous not only for the musical experience but for the frequent costume changes, with her parading as if on the catwalk at a fashion show. She was voted Best Dressed Woman in 1993 by the Hong Kong Fashion Design Association.

By the end of the eighties, Anita had become so famous that she decided to renounce all music awards after 1990. During her 1991-92 tour, she announced what was to be her farewell concert, although she would still appear for charity campaigns. Movie mogul Run Run Shaw pledged to donate half

Pre-Trio days

Top:
Follow the Star

Above:
Till We
Meet Again

Right:
Scared Stiff

a million dollars if Anita would sing *An Old Friend Coming* during one benefit concert. Needless to say she did, and the concert raised almost HK$38 million.

In addition to this tremendously successful musical career, Anita was also carving out a name for herself in the movies. She started with an appearance in *Crazy '83* (1983), and after several other minor roles starred alongside Chow Yun Fat in *A Hundred Ways To Murder Your Wife*, playing the bitchy wife of Kenny Bee. She appeared alongside Chow Yun Fat again in *Scared Stiff* (1987) playing

Top:
Saviour of
the Soul

Above and left:
A selection of
shots from
Rouge with
her co-star
Leslie Cheung

Top:
Miracles, with Jackie Chan

Above:
Dressed to kill in A Better Tomorrow 3

Below:
My Father is a Hero

the victim of a serial killer, with Chow as the killer himself! But it was the haunting *Rouge*, made in the same year, that was finally to give Anita the kind of acting role she deserved. Directed by Stanley Kwan, *Rouge* cast Anita alongside up and coming star Leslie Cheung and Alex Man, for once hanging up his guns to play the more sympathetic role of a journalist helping her in her quest to find the lost love of her life. Master Twelve (Cheung) had failed to honour their suicide pact fifty years earlier, leaving her spirit to wander aimlessly in a bid to rekindle their love in the afterlife.

In 1989, Anita played a singer opposite Jackie Chan in Miracles, aka *Mr Canton and Lady Rose*. She also starred with Chow Yun Fat again in the underrated *A Better Tomorrow 3: Love and Death in Saigon*. This time her performance was more geared towards the action genre than previous roles, and it has to be said, she carries it off brilliantly. Although some people find the film slower than the first two parts due to director Tsui Hark's excessive use of slow-mo, his camerawork does showcase Anita's performance as a battling babe very impressively.

In 1990, Anita displayed her abilty to shine as a martial artist when she was cast alongside two of the major contributors to the genre, Samo Hung and Yuen Biao, in *Shanghai, Shanghai*. Despite this awesome weight of talent, the film is quite disappointing, and Anita really steals the film with her fighting flair. There are two outstanding scenes, one a ballroom dancing

sequence with Yuen Biao, the other a sexually charged
fight scene with Anita doing some mindboggling aerial
kicking in a centresplit dress under the watchful eye of a
slow motion camera.

Without doubt one of Anita's most enjoyable roles
came in 1991, with *Saviour of the Soul*. She plays twin
sisters, one vying for the love of Andy Lau, the other a
neurotic inventor of crazy gimmicks like the 'breathless
bullet'. It is a superbly stylish movie that gives Anita's fans
a double dose of their fave babe playing both great action
and comedy.

Throughout the nineties, Anita has appeared in the kind
of A grade movies which have pushed her movie
career to a similar level of success as her musical
career. Apart from establishing herself alongside
Chow Yun Fat in the eighties, she has
appeared with many top box office stars
including Chow Sing Chi (*Justice My
Foot*, 1992, *Fight Back to School 3*,
1993) and Jackie Chan (*Drunken Master
2*, 1994, *Rumble in the Bronx*, 1995). In fact one of her
best comedy roles yet is as Jackie's feisty mother in
Drunken Master 2, even though she's actually ten years
younger than him! She
steals every scene, and
it's just a pity she
doesn't get to show off
her fighting skills with
Jackie. She also stars
alongside Jet Lee in *My*

Father is a Hero (1994).

Despite having such a broad repertoire of roles, Anita is best known in the UK as a femme fatale, due to the superb double bill of *The Heroic Trio* and *Heroic Trio 2: Executioners* (both 1993). Their release onto the UK market has increased her audience tenfold and has started many of her fans backtracking to find earlier works which are available on video in the UK.

Anita appeared in the UK during her farewell tour, and since she has decided to continue with her recording career as well as her movie projects, should she choose to perform in the UK again there would doubtless be many western faces among the audience. Part of her wide appeal must be her unusual, atypically Chinese looks, with full lips and the ability to change her appearance constantly. She can look very sexy, and her raunchy, rebellious image certainly adds to her charisma. However, it is her outstanding acting ability, enabling her to play such a diverse range of roles, that has endeared her to critics and audiences alike. To sum Anita up is quite easily – she's stunning, sexy and *very* talented. We can only hope to see a great many more of

Top: Moon Warriors

Above: A Better Tomorrow 3

Right: Rumble in the Bronx

Anita Mui being silly in Drunken Master 2

MUI-ography
Anita Mui / Mui Yim Fong

梅艷芳

1983	Crazy '83
	Let's Make Laugh
	A Week of Passion
1984	Fate
	Musical Singer
	Behind the Yellow Line
1985	Song and Dance
	Good Luck to You
	Young Cops
1986	A Hundred Ways To Murder Your Wife
	Inspector Chocolate
	Last Song in Paris
	Why Why Tell Me
	Happy Din Don
1987	Scared Stiff
	Happy Bigamist
	Happy Stories
	Lucky Diamond
	Rouge
	One Husband Too Many
1988	The Greatest Lover
	Destiny
	Stage Door Johnny
	The Evil Ghost

1989	Miracles aka Mr Canton and Lady Rose
	A Better Tomorrow 3
	Shanghai, Shanghai
	The Yuppie Fantasia
198?	Follow the Star
198?	Till We Meet Again
198?	Trouble Couples
1990	Last Princess of Manchuria
	Kawashima Yoshiko
	Fortune Code
1991	Saviour of the Soul
	Au Revoir Mon Amour
	The Banquet
	The Top Bet
1992	Justice My Foot
	Moon Warriors
1993	Fight Back to School 3
	The Magic Crane
	The Heroic Trio
	Heroic Trio 2: Executioners
1994	Drunken Master 2
1995	Rumble in the Bronx
	My Father is a Hero

楊紫瓊

MICHELLE YEOH

'beautiful vase made of iron and steel'

"To become a successful actress in the kung fu genre requires more than good looks and a smidgeon of acting, it requires attitude, and Michelle Yeoh, like her male counterparts, regards danger as a challenge. It is this outlook that has earned her the name Gang Tai Hua Ping: beautiful vase made of iron and steel." — Aking Wong

Born in Ipoh, Malaysia and university educated in England, Michelle Yeoh – who like Maggie Cheung, speaks perfect English – is in my opinion the queen of the battling babes. She was the first of the modern day femme fatales to come to the attention of the British public, under the name Michelle Khan, when Screen Entertainment released the now rare and collectable Police Assassins (1986) in late 1987 or early 1988 onto the UK video market. Originally entitled Royal Warriors, this was the second part in the long running In the Line of Duty saga.

This exceptional star of Hong Kong action films had no previous martial arts experience, but her early penchant for dance made up for her lack of knowledge of fighting. She did not grow up with the desire to become an actress. She was actually considering starting a ballet school in Malaysia when she won the Miss Malaysia beauty contest at the age of 21, a title which admirers of her screen work will surely agree was well deserved. Again,

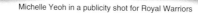
Michelle Yeoh in a publicity shot for Royal Warriors

this was not an intentional career move: her mother sent some photographs in to the contest, and when Michelle was asked to go along to the semi-finals she went just to stop her mum nagging her about it!

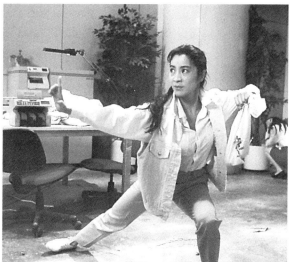

Above: Project S action showcase

During Michelle's time in England she studied ballet, jazz and contemporary dance. This experience has proved a sound foundation for other action babes including Moon Lee and Cynthia Khan. Michelle had done some professional dancing before she sustained an injury and decided to return to her studies. She was advised never to do anything physical again – presumably her doctor has never seen the stunts she pulls off in her movies!

In 1984 Michelle got the opportunity to do a commercial for D&B Films, opposite Jackie Chan, who was the first person she ever worked with in Hong Kong. On the strength of that, she was signed exclusively to D&B to star in several movies. Her first was *Owl Versus Bumbo* (1985) for director Samo Hung. Shortly afterwards she starred in *Yes, Madam* (1985), released in the UK as *Police Assassins 2*. This was American femme fatale

Michelle Yeoh with Cynthia Rothrock in Police Assassins 2, aka Yes Madam and In the Line of Duty

Cynthia Rothrock's first film, and the two became friends. *Yes, Madam*, directed by the underrated Yuen Kwai (Corey Yuen), was a very successful showcase for Michelle's action ability. Although it has very little plot, the eighty percent action quota has proved a

Michelle Yeoh showcases her talents alongside Jackie Chan in Police Story 3: Supercop, shot on location in Kuala Lumpar, Malaysia, Michelle's native country

firm favourite with UK fans. However, there is one key fight scene cut out of the final print; D&B have a show reel of it which was viewed several years ago by several people I know. There is also a scene change in the English release. In the opening sequence of the original version, Michelle slams a book shut on the private parts of a flasher. In the UK version, this scene is replaced by the opening sequence of Samo Hung's movie *Where's Officer Tuba?* It is a more dramatic opening for the movie, but nonetheless not a version for completists.

Following the success of *Yes, Madam* throughout Asia, Michelle reprised her feisty femme fatale role in *Royal Warriors* (1986). Michelle is a perfectionist and was encouraged to learn martial arts on the set from instructors and choreographers, hoping to make her fighting as authentic as possible. Consequently her performance improved dramatically. She said, "I try my best. Other people have given me the opportunity and I will not disappoint them."

It was during the filming that Michelle suffered the first of many on set injuries, dislocating her shoulder. The stunt coordinator had one of the guys kick her so hard it made her fall badly, knocking her shoulder out. The pain was so bad it kept her awake for seven nights, and during this time she was filming continuously. Not surprisingly, she swore she'd never make an action film again, although luckily for her fans, she soon changed her mind.

Royal Warriors was a great success, and with her first two major action movies achieving sales outside Asia, finding their way onto the video shelves of many European nations (in some territories they were retitled *Ultra Force* 1 and 2) Michelle was becoming a name to reckon with.

Now Michelle had two starring roles under her belt her presence was beginning to be strongly felt, not only for her fighting ability and gutsy attitude to doing her own stunts but also the fact that she brought a likeable personality to the parts she played. She next started work on *Magnificent Warriors* in 1987, which was originally scheduled to be completed in Taiwan in three weeks but actually took a very tiring three months to finish. She was back in battling babe mode, doing fight scenes almost every day, and sustaining further injuries. "I was exhausted," she has said, "however I would urge myself to work harder. After all, as a performer you are part of a team and have to keep going despite injuries." Her formidable opponent was Wong Jan Lee, whose hard fighting techniques had already taken out several of Jackie Chan's teeth while filming *Snake in the Eagle's Shadow*. *Magnificent Warriors*, which is also available in the UK, allowed Michelle to bring another exhilarating action flick to the screen, although in my opinion it's not as fine as her previous two action outings.

Still recovering from her injuries, her next movie, *Easy Money* (1988) contained far less action. Presumably this is why it has never been released in the UK. I remember going to see it on the Chinatown circuit, hoping to see another dazzling display of Michelle's ability, only to discover it was a drama loosely based on Steve McQueen's *Thomas Crown Affair*. Michelle brought plenty of glamour, but little fighting to the movie, which was partly shot on location in the UK. Bey Logan was on set to interview her for *Combat* magazine, and without a doubt it was him giving her front cover of a national magazine which not only

This page:

Top:

A still from the missing action scene cut from the original release of Police Assassins 2, aka Yes Madam

Middle and Bottom:

Police Story 3 promotional artwork, prominently featuring Michelle Yeoh

Back to tradition for a new wave of kung fu movies

Top and inset:

Wing Chun

Below:

Michelle Yeoh delivers a fine performance alongside Jet Lee in Tai Chi Master

it was good news for fans that she was back to work in 1992, opting to make a comeback in the huge box office smash *Police Story 3: Supercop* alongside her old friend Jackie Chan. This was also the first time she appeared in a movie with Maggie Cheung. The movie, which is available in the UK, was directed by Stanley Tong, who had also directed *Magnificent Warriors*.

Michelle's four year absence from the screen had not diminished her skill. Under Jackie's experienced guidance, she performed the famous motorcycle stunt which must have stunned Hong Kong's hardened stuntmen with its difficulty. As you can see from the outtakes at the end of the film, Michelle performed the

widened her fan base in the UK but put her firmly on the map as the number one female action star.

At this stage in Michelle's career she married D&B owner and producer Dickson Poon in 1988 and went into semi-retirement, leaving the way clear for rising femme fatale stars like Cynthia Khan to fill her shoes. Sadly the marriage didn't work out, although

Michelle Yeoh with former husband Dickson Poon, head of D&B Films

Michelle Yeoh with Jet Lee

Left: Michelle is set for action in the stylishly shot Butterfly and Sword

Below:

A rare publicity shot of Michelle for Dragon Gate Inn. Sadly she was never to star in it and was later replaced by Maggie Cheung

stunt without the aid of wires, and it is most certainly her and not a stand in. The film is now to be released theatrically in the US by Miramax, which is sure to increase her already huge army of fans there.

Michelle was then signed to star in the Tsui Hark production *Dragon Gate Inn*, but dropped out and was replaced by Maggie Cheung. Instead she made the Golden Harvest film *Project S* (1993), which also had a cameo from Jackie Chan. Michelle's career was right back on track, and 1993 was a great year for her, with fine performances in Yuen Woo Ping's *Wing Chun* alongside Donnie Yen, Johnny To's *Heroic Trio* and *Heroic Trio 2: Executioners* which were shot almost back to back, and Wong Jing's superb *Holy Weapon* aka *Seven Maidens*. She also made an American based film called *Fist of Steel*.

In 1994 Michelle joined forces with superstar Jet Lee in the impressive *Tai Chi*

Master. She also made the visually stunning *Butterfly and Sword* (aka *Comet, Butterfly and Sword*), a superb fantasy swordplay movie co-starring Tony Leung, Donnie Yen and Joey Wong.

In 1995 Michelle was approached by John Woo while in the US as a possible candidate for the *Once A Thief* TV series. She couldn't commit to a full series, but in a recent

conversation John told me he had high hopes that she would break into the US market and he still hopes to do a project with her. It has also been rumoured that Oliver Stone has shown interest in her. She was considered for a part in Jean-Claude Van Damme's *Street Fighter*, but lost out to the *Joy Luck Club*'s Ming-Na Wen. However, it seems likely that like many other Hong Kong stars, she will soon make a name for herself in the US.

Recently Michelle has completed a new action flick, *The Story of Stunt Women Ah Gum*, which is about to be released as we go to print, also starring Samo Hung, and starred in *The Sung Dynasty*

Family alongside Maggie Cheung. This was a more serious drama role for Michelle, who despite being a dynamic action babe is keen to pursue more weighty roles. In the future she hopes to win more challenging roles that stretch her acting, as well as action roles. She would like to work with Chow Yun Fat, and also overseas stars she admires like Schwarzenegger, Stallone, De Niro and Nicholson. With the current trend towards Hong Kong movies in the west, it's not impossible that she will achieve her dream. I've never been fortunate enough to interview Michelle, but recently while in a hotel lobby in Hong Kong she walked past my table, and I have to say she looked better than ever, radiating a presence stronger than any other Hong Kong actress I've seen. Michelle is currently enjoying success in the USA with the release of *Police Story 3: Supercop*, which opened in July. Let's hope there is a great future in store for her.

Top and Bottom:
Two of the more unpleasant moments for Michelle – Heroic Trio and Heroic Trio 2: Executioners…
Above:
Michelle gets serious with Jackie in Police Story 3: Supercop

YEOH-ography
Michelle Yeoh / Michelle Khan / Yeung Chi King

楊紫瓊

1985	Owl Versus Bumbo
	In the Line of Duty aka Yes Madam aka Police Assassins 2
	Twinkle Twinkle Lucky Stars
1986	In the Line of Duty 2 aka Police Assassins aka Royal Warriors
1988	Magnificent Warriors
	Easy Money
1992	Police Story 3: Supercop
1993	Wing Chun
	Project S
	The Heroic Trio
	Heroic Trio 2: Executioners
	Holy Weapon aka Seven Maidens
	Fist of Steel
1994	Tai Chi Master
	Butterfly and Sword
	Wonder 7
1996	Stunt Women Ah Gum
	Sung Dynasty Family

CYNTHIA KHAN

楊麗青

"GET OUT A' MY FACE!!"
Cynthia Khan pole axes Michael Woods
– In The Line of Duty 4: Witness

in the line of duty

cynthia khan

text:
Rick Baker

A stunning publicity shot for Angel on Fire

Cynthia Khan (Yeung Lai Ching) is a Taiwanese beauty who was brought to the forefront as a replacement for kung fu actress Michelle Khan/Yeoh. As always in Asia, marketable names come first, and it seems her moniker was created by D&B Films taking the Christian name of Cynthia Rothrock and the surname of Michelle Khan (as she was then known), making a double-bladed name to lure the audience in.

Like many of her contemporaries, Cynthia's dream was to become a dancer. "I thought of becoming a dance teacher and going abroad to learn more about dancing, but I twisted my waist during a rehearsal and my doctor suggested that it would be difficult to continue a career in dancing," she has said. It

Cynthia Khan poses for the cameras.

Right:

Cynthia in Mary Quant pose for It's Now or Never

Below:

The casual girl about town look

was that cruel twist of fate that put Cynthia on the road to film stardom. The daughter of a jeweller, Cynthia had been studying jazz ballet, traditional Chinese, modern and Spanish dance since she was ten. At seventeen she won the new talent award in a national competition organised by one of the TV stations. But her parents wanted her to read management studies at a Taipei university. In order to get her own way, she went on hunger strike. Her parents eventually gave in and allowed her to enter an arts institute in Taipei. Her future looked good, and she would probably have realised her ambition to become a dance teacher if she hadn't been injured. For a short while she pursued a singing career, though not with any notable success.

Many of the female stars in this book could be called attractive and sexy, but Cynthia Khan really is an outstandingly stunning woman. It was probably these radiant looks that made Golden Horse award winning director Chang Yi offer her the second lead role in his movie *My True Love* (1987). Ironically, in the movie she plays a dance teacher. The film enjoyed only mediocre success but the cinemagoers and critics noticed this eyecatching beauty, noted at the time as 'a new blood with great potential'. Shortly afterwards, she made an appearance in a low budget

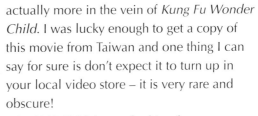
It's all In the
Line of Duty
for Cynthia

fantasy horror flick made in Taiwan, *The Three Headed Monster.* It sounds like a Godzilla type movie but it is actually more in the vein of *Kung Fu Wonder Child.* I was lucky enough to get a copy of this movie from Taiwan and one thing I can say for sure is don't expect it to turn up in your local video store – it is very rare and obscure!

In 1987 D&B began looking for a replacement for Michelle Khan. There was no shortage of candidates, but after checking out more than a hundred wannabe action stars,

In the Line of
Duty 5:
Middle Man

Right:
Cynthia with
co-star David Wu
in a publicity shot

Below:
With rising star

the talent team saw Cynthia in *My True Love.* She said, "I was overjoyed at receiving a film offer from a Hong Kong film company. But that night I had to start a revolution at home by convincing my parents that the venture was worthy. Obviously, like all parents, they were going to be a bit worried about me going alone to a strange place with no relatives to take care of me. But I convinced them to give me a chance for two years."

Cynthia was to find it daunting and difficult to step into Michelle Khan's kung fu footsteps, as Michelle had so quickly established herself as an action star in the cop blockbuster *Yes Madam* (1985). Cynthia said, "People called me the heir of the Inspector Madam (referring to Michelle) but I didn't set out to imitate anybody, although I watched all of Michelle's films. But I think it's unfair to compare me with Michelle. Once the people had accepted Michelle as a kung fu actress then they tended to demand more of me before I could be accepted."

But it wasn't long before Cynthia established herself as a feisty femme. Her big break
came in the third part of the *In The Line Of
Duty* series (released in the UK as *Force of the
Dragon*). She quickly moved on to make part
four, known in Hong Kong as *Witness* (1988),
with Donnie Yen. For me this is still one of
the classic modern day kung fu flicks of the
eighties, with director Yuen Woo Ping getting
maximum performances from all the cast. His
skill as a martial arts director really sharpened
up Cynthia's overall performance, especially
in terms of her fighting – even though, as in
all her D&B films, the acting comes well
down the list in importance, after glamour
and kung fu.

After the success of *Witness*, Cynthia
teamed up with Donnie and Yuen Woo Ping
again for the superb *Tiger Cage 2* (1989). It's
worth noting that there are two versions of
this movie. In the Chinese version, available
in the UK from Made in Hong Kong, we get
the original ending with Donnie fighting
Robin Shou, with a little help from Rosamund

Above:
Middle Man
Below:
The bogus In the
Line of Duty film
Queen's High,
aka In the Line
of Duty –
The Beginning

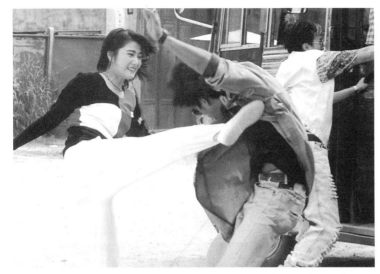

This page: Non-stop action for Cynthia in Pink Bomb

Kwan and a piece of 4x2. In the Malaysian version or English dubbed version, released in the UK by Imperial, the end sequence has Cynthia fighting Robin Shou. In Malaysia the ends of movies are quite often changed (most notably, Bruce Lee's *Game of Death*) because anyone who has done something bad, even if they are the hero, cannot be shown to get away without punishment. What a law abiding nation!

Cynthia continued to play the woman cop avenger in the *In The Line Of Duty* series, which went on for three more parts under her D&B contract: number five, *Middle Man* (1990), number six, *Forbidden Arsenal* (1991) and number seven, *Sea Wolves* (1991). She also made another film for D&B in 1991, *Queen's High*, which featured a wedding dress clad, two-Uzi-toting Khan wreaking havoc after the slaughter of her husband on her wedding day. Confusingly, the press book issued by D&B for this movie called it *In The Line Of Duty: The Beginning*, which was obviously intended to cash in on the success of the series, even though the movie was totally unrelated.

Throughout the nineties, Cynthia's career has remained active. When D&B stopped making movies in early 1992 her versatile fighting skills allowed her to make the

Cynthia gets
dressed to wed
as the uzi-toting
bride in
Queen's High

transition to the new wave swordplay genre, playing the lead in *Zen of Sword* (1992), a film described as the follow-up to King Hu's classic *Touch of Zen*. In 1993 she made *13 Cold Blooded Eagles*, and following the success of Jackie Chan's *City Hunter* she was cast as his female equivalent in *Madam City Hunter*.

In the UK, Cynthia's popularity is on a similar level to that enjoyed by Moon Lee and Yukari Oshima. She is still making movies, shooting more often now in Taiwan than Hong Kong. During 1995 and '96 she has turned more towards TV, although between that busy schedule she is still making feature length films, often produced by our friends at Filmswell International. Although these get a theatrical release in Taiwan and the Philippines, they seem to go straight to video in Hong Kong and global Chinatowns. Cynthia recently

Left:
Cynthia Khan
poses for 13
Cold Blooded
Eagles

the essential guide to deadly china dolls • **111**

Cynthia Khan gets to grips with the enemy in Avenging Quartet

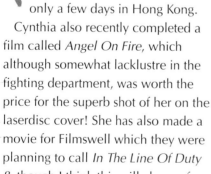

Avenging Quartet

returned to the big screen alongside Yuen Biao in *The Tough Beauty and the Sloppy Slop*. I can't imagine how they thought this name could be marketable in the west! I suspect there was an error in translation and it should be called Sloppy Cop! Sadly the film closed after only a few days in Hong Kong. Cynthia also recently completed a film called *Angel On Fire*, which although somewhat lacklustre in the fighting department, was worth the price for the superb shot of her on the laserdisc cover! She has also made a movie for Filmswell which they were planning to call *In The Line Of Duty 8*, though I think this will change for the international market.

Despite this downturn in her career in Hong Kong, Cynthia's movies are still very popular sellers in Europe, and with movies like *Witness*, *Queen's High* and the undisputed modern day classic *Tiger Cage 2* available, Cynthia's profile will always remain impressive in the west.

Middle:
Queen's High
Right:
Tough Beauty and the Sloppy Slop (sic), with Yuen Biao

KHAN-ography 楊麗青

Cynthia Khan / Yeung Lai Ching

1987	My True Love
	The Three Headed Monster
	In the Line of Duty 3: Force of the Dragon
1988	In the Line of Duty 4: Witness
1989	Tiger Cage 2
1990	In the Line of Duty 5: Middle Man
1991	In the Line of Duty 6: Forbidden Arsenal
	In the Line of Duty 7: Sea Wolves
	Queen's High
1992	Zen of Sword
	Avenging Quartet
	Dead End of Besiegers
	A Serious Shock: Yes Madam 2 aka Death Triangle
	Eternal Fist
1993	13 Cold Blooded Eagles
	Madam City Hunter
	Pink Bomb
	It's Now or Never
	The Gods Must Be Crazy 3
	The Inspector Wears a Skirt 4
1995	Ultimate Revenge
1996	Angel on Fire
	Tough Beauty and the Sloppy Slop
	In the Line of Duty 8

Dead End of Besiegers

SIBELLE HU

胡慧中

"SOFT ON THE OUTSIDE, A FIGHTING FURY UNDERNEATH THE FACE OF A HUNDRED FEMME FATALE FILMS"

lights, camera, action!

sibelle hu

Sibelle Hu kicks some ass in Deadly China Dolls, aka Lethal Panther

text:
Rick Baker

Queen of Gamble

Sibelle Hu (Hu Hui Chung) was born on May 4, 1958. Her name may not be that familiar to western audiences, but if you've seen a reasonable number of Hong Kong movies you will almost certainly have seen her. She was until recently one of the most active actresses around, and is often associated with other popular action actresses like Moon Lee and Yukari Oshima. In fact, for a woman with such an extensive back catalogue of movies there seems to be remarkably little known in the west about Sibelle Hu.

In fact, Sibelle has appeared in so many movies (over two hundred, by some estimates!) that it would be a daunting task to try to provide a complete filmography, especially as there are so many movies in which she either makes a cameo appearance, or footage of her has simply

been edited in. One can only assume her name must have incredible pulling power for audiences in some territories. Films like the

Eastern Heroes release *Deadly China Dolls* (aka *Lethal Panther*, 1991) for example, have Sibelle cut in for the opening scene and at various points throughout the movie, and director Godfrey Ho confirmed that she was only on set for one or two days, to lend the kudos of her name to the cast. Despite her limited screen time in many movies, you can always find her name in the top three credits

Top: The Dragon Fighters

Above: Sibelle in mercenary pose for Deadly China Dolls

Right: Sibelle gets serious in Devil Huntress

Below right: Crystal Hunt

Her movie career then took a break, and one may assume that during this hiatus she was doing TV work of some description. But after her appearance in *My Little Yellow* (1984) her film career went into overdrive.

Those who have watched any quantity of Sibelle's films will know that she is more often than not typecast as a gun-toting cop, but she has received critical acclaim for her performances,

of any film her face has graced. One might almost describe her as an exploitation actress!

Sibelle first found fame when she starred in the feature film *Kwun Han* (1978) at the tender age of nineteen, making her second film, *Your Smiling Face*, later that same year.

most notably alongside Jackie Chan in *My Lucky Stars* (1985) and with Sam Hui in *Inspector Chocolate* (1988). Her tough screen persona paid dividends when she was elected as one of the top ten Asian stars in Korea. She has also won Best Actress at the Hundred

would find photo showcases from her latest movie in virtually every edition, and often her face adorning the front cover too.

Sibelle has starred alongside some of Hong Kong's greats, including Jackie Chan (*My Lucky Stars*, 1985, *Twinkle Twinkle Lucky Stars*, 1986), Chow Yun Fat (*The Occupant*, 1984, *The Seventh Curse*, 1986), Chow Sing Chi (*Sleazy Dizzy*, 1990) and Jet Lee (*Fong Sai Yuk*, 1993). She also starred in a martial art movie for Shaw Brothers, *The Master Strikes Back* (1985) with Ti Lung. More recently Sibelle's career has been harder to track, and it seems she has eased up after the hectic filming schedule she has maintained over the last ten years. For those of you wishing to check out this deadly doll, there is a good selection of her films available in the UK, which will give you the opportunity to gauge whether she's the femme fatale for you. The obvious choices are *My Lucky Stars* and *Twinkle Twinkle Lucky Stars*, and the Cynthia Rothrock vehicle *Top Squad* (aka *The Inspector Wears A Skirt*). *Deadly China Dolls* (aka *Lethal Panther*), *Holy Virgin Versus the Evil Dead* and *Dreaming the Reality* are also available.

Top:
Sibelle versus Samo in Bury Me High

Above and Bottom right:
Combat at Heaven's Gate

Right: Sibelle surveys the carnage in Fighting Fists

Flowers Awards in China, although to western fans her fighting style seems less 'screen pretty' than that of Moon Lee or Yukari Oshima. Sibelle has certainly experienced intense popularity in Hong Kong, where a column of *Cinemart* magazine was dedicated to her and at one stage you

SIBELLE-ography

Sibelle Hu / Hu Hui Chung

胡慧中

1978	Kwun Han
	Your Smiling Face
	I Love Lolando
1980	Kung Hai Fat Choi
1982	A Dog's Life
	My Little Yellow
1984	The Occupant
1985	The Master Strikes Back
	My Lucky Stars
1986	The Seventh Curse
	Twinkle Twinkle Lucky Stars
1987	Crazy Spirit
1988	The Inspector Wears a Skirt
	aka Top Squad
	Inspector Chocolate
	Haunted Madam
1989	The Inspector Wears a Skirt 2
	Devil Huntress
	The Yuppie Fantasia
	To Spy With Love
	Thunder Squad
	The Seventh Curse
1990	Sleazy Dizzy
	Holy Virgin Versus the Evil Dead
	China Heat
	Magic Amethyst
	The Gamble Goddess
	To Spy With Love
	The Dragon Fighters
	Raid On Royal Casino Marine
	Fire Phoenix

1991	Drugs Area
	The Queen of Gamble
	The Roar of the Vietnamese
	Bury Me High
	Fatal Mission
	Deadly China Dolls
	aka Lethal Panther
	Crystal Hunt
1992	The Mighty Gambler
	All's Well That Ends Well
	Lethal Contact
	Way of the Lady Boxers
	Japanese Katano
	Emergency Police Lady
1993	Combat at Heaven's Gate
	Angel Terminators 2
	The Big Deal
	Fong Sai Yuk
	Fighting Fists
	Dreaming the Reality
1994	Angel Project
1996	Tai Chi Master 2

王祖賢

"Slender figure, pale face and long straigght, silky hair, she was destined to become a major Hong Kong movie star"

This page: Joey Wong in A Chinese Ghost Story

ghost in the machine

joey wong

text:
**Rick
Baker**

Joey Wong (aka Joey Wang, Wong Tsu Hsien) was born in Taiwan on January 31, 1967. She cut her teeth in her first movie, *The Lakeside is Cold*, that same year. She was schooled at the Kwo Gwong Chinese School of Performing Arts, and moved to Hong Kong in 1984, at the age of seventeen. With her tall, slender figure, pale face and long, straight, silky hair, she was destined to become a major Hong Kong movie star.

Joey Wong in
fashion pose

around the world, although it's famous more for its extraordinary story than its cast. Having said that, it did bring Joey overnight fame elsewhere in the world.

In 1985, Joey made the first film of her adult career for Shaw Brothers, a sequel called *Let's Make Laugh 2*. In the same year she appeared with Sam Hui in *Working Class*. Now her career was beginning to get established and in 1986 she made a further six movies, including *Where's Officer Tuba?* with Samo Hung, and *A Hundred Ways to Murder Your Wife* with Chow Yun Fat. 1987's *A Chinese Ghost Story*, produced by Tsui Hark, made her a superstar. Not only did the critically acclaimed movie put her on the map in Hong Kong, Korea and Japan, but it also established her as the ghostly face of Chinese cinema, an identity in which she has become to some extent typecast.

A Chinese Ghost Story

Despite her haunting beauty, Joey Wong is not a household name in the UK, maybe because she is an actress rather than an action star and packs a presence, not a punch. Although not many of her films are available in the UK, at the end of the eighties we were lucky enough to have *A Chinese Ghost Story* screened on BBC2. This has become a cult movie in most territories

A Chinese
Ghost Story 2

In 1988 she reprised her ghostly persona for Golden Harvest in *Portrait of A Nymph*, alongside Yuen Biao. Despite its cast and backing, it was merely a pale imitation of *A Chinese Ghost Story*. However, it was a successful year for Joey. She also had a small role in the Tsui Hark produced gangster classic *The Big Heat*, and starred again alongside Chow Yun Fat, himself the box office king, in *Fractured Follies* and *The Diary of a Big Man*. In this year she also made a movie Hong Kong critics regard as one of her best works, *Law of Justice*.

In 1989 the film work kept on flooding in. She once again rehashed her ghostly image for *Reincarnation of Golden Lotus*, and appeared alongside Kenny Bee in the excellent *My Heart is That Eternal Rose*, directed by Patrick Tam, which can be seen at the front of Toby Russell's documentary *Cinema of Vengeance*. The crowning point of the year was Wong Jing casting her with Chow Yun Fat in the box office smash *God of Gamblers*.

A Chinese Ghost Story showcase:

Top left: Joey Wong takes flight in A Chinese Ghost Story

Centre: A pensive Joey in A Chinese Ghost Story

Other pictures: A Chinese Ghost Story 3

Top:

Butterfly and Sword

Top right:

Two Eagles
Shooting Heroes

Middle:

Portrait of a Nymph

Below:

Joey needs snake
eyes in the back of
her head to keep
out of trouble in
Green Snake

The phenomenal success of this movie made Joey as huge a star as Chow Yun Fat in Hong Kong, Korea and Japan, and she was so in demand that she made almost a dozen films in 1990. Despite her immense popularity, it seems she would not turn a script down! Her roles vary in quality from low budget movies like *Cyprus Tigers*, *Point of No Return* and *An Eye For An Eye* to big budget productions like Wong Jing's *The Big Score* and *A Chinese Ghost Story 2*. Even with this hectic schedule, she still found time to come to London to make *Killer's Romance* for Regent Films, with Simon Yam.

1991 remained busy, with Joey making the third part of the *A Chinese Ghost Story* trilogy, and exploiting her ghostly image in a further four films that year, in *An Eternal Combat* with Lam Ching Ying, in *Fantasy Romance* with Tony Leung, in *A Chinese Legend* with Jacky Cheung and in the Wu Ma directed *Fox*

City Hunter

My Heart is that Eternal Rose with Kenny Bee

Legend, aka *Moon Legend*. She also appeared with a cast of hundreds in *The Banquet*.

The following year her workload decreased quite dramatically, although notable roles included *Casino Tycoon* parts one and two, with Andy Lau. 1993 showed an improvement of quality over quantity, as Joey starred in the frantic, fast paced *Two Eagles Shooting Heroes*, put in a very erotic performance alongside screen beauty Maggie Cheung in Tsui Hark's *Green Snake*, joined Brigitte Lin for *Swordsman 3: The East is Red* and played a sexy gun-toting agent in Jackie Chan's *City Hunter*.

Sadly, since then Joey seems to have taken a break from movie making. Her picture still regularly appears in Hong Kong magazines like *Cinemart*, and rumours have circulated in Taiwan

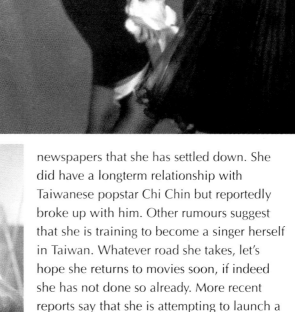
Joey Wong ltakes charge in City Hunter

newspapers that she has settled down. She did have a longterm relationship with Taiwanese popstar Chi Chin but reportedly broke up with him. Other rumours suggest that she is training to become a singer herself in Taiwan. Whatever road she takes, let's hope she returns to movies soon, if indeed she has not done so already. More recent reports say that she is attempting to launch a singing career in Japan.

Swordsman 3: The East is Red

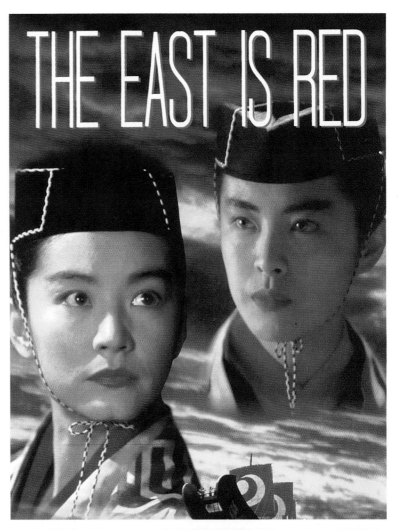

THE EAST IS RED

Top: Joey Wong and Maggie Cheung in a dramatic moment from Green Snake

Above: Kung Fu Versus Acrobatic, with Andy Lau

Below: Joey poses again for the cameras

Middle right: Joey Wong with Leslie Cheung in Two Eagles Shooting Heroes

Below right: Joey Wong poses in flash car in City Hunter

JOEY-ography

Joey Wong / Wong Tsu Hsien

王祖賢

Green Snake

BRIGITTE LIN

林青霞

The Bride With White Hair

invincible asia

brigitte lin

Zu: Warriors From the Magic Mountain

text:
Toby Russell

Brigitte Lin (Lin Chin Hsia, also known as Venus Lin due to her beauty) was born in Southern Taiwan on November 23, 1956. She is regarded as the greatest beauty on the Chinese film screen, and those who have seen her new wave movies in the nineties will find it easy to see why she has been granted this accolade.

After graduating from high school she was noticed by a film director in 1973 when she accompanied a friend who was auditioning for a movie. The director was captivated by Brigitte's classic beauty and even though she had no intention of becoming an actress she found herself starring in the movie, playing a schoolgirl.

Brigitte quickly became hot property in Taiwan, often playing a similar type of role. Her screen persona made her the second most popular love story actress, after Lin Fong Chiao (former wife of Jackie Chan), who held the top spot for most of the seventies. In 1980 she went to America to study Integrated Art,

Brigitte is waiting for her men in Chungking Express

then moved back to Taiwan for a short stint in action pictures like *The Seven Foxes, Golden Queen Commando, Fantasy Mission Force* and *Pink Force Commando*.

Producer/director and sometime actor Tsui Hark was eager to use her talents in the 1982 classic *Zu: Warriors From the Magic Mountain*, in which she gave a memorable performance. *Zu: Warriors* was to become a massive box office success and Tsui Hark cast her again in 1983, in *All the Wrong Spies*.

Top: Dragon Gate Inn

Above: Brigitte Lin tries some pretty drastic martial arts techniques in Night Orchid

Right: Brigitte Lin is the Ice Maiden in Zu: Warriors From the Magic Mountain

Be Careful Sweetheart

Demi Gods and Semi Devils

Zu: Warriors From the
Magic Mountain

Kung fu superstar Jackie Chan then approached Brigitte to star in his critically acclaimed box office smash *Police Story* (1985). Brigitte plays the girlfriend of crime boss Chu Yuen and is eventually persuaded to turn queen's evidence against him. The role proved particularly challenging for Brigitte as danger comes with the territory when you star in a Jackie Chan movie, and she undertook some pretty dangerous stunts which confirmed her status as an action babe. She knew what she was letting herself in for, as she had already worked with Jackie in 1982, on *Fantasy Mission Force*.

Her working relationship with Tsui Hark then continued in the huge hit *Peking Opera Blues* (1986) in which she starred alongside Sally Yeh and Cherrie Chung. The movie was an international success, playing in festivals all over the world.

Part of Brigitte's appeal lies in her versatility

Zu: Warriors

as an actress who can handle action roles and more challenging storylines with equal panache. She remained busy throughout the eighties in popular movies like *True Colours* (1986) with Ti Lung, *The Lady in Black* (1987) and *Web of Deception* (1989). But it was in the nineties that the western audience became aware of her, as the new wave martial art movie scene began to flourish and her high-wire fighting femme persona was established, building upon the techniques which Tsui Hark had already experimented with in *Zu: Warrors* a decade earlier.

Her charismatic performances in *Dragon Gate Inn* (1992), produced by Tsui Hark, and alongside Chow Sing Chi in *Royal Tramp* parts 1 and 2 (both 1992) made her the ideal choice to play the transsexual Japanese pirate and vicious warrior Invincible Asia, starring with Jet Lee in the huge box office smash *Swordsman 2* (1992). With the help of a book, Invincible Asia develops devastating internal power which allows him to transform into a woman. This role was reprised in *Swordsman 3: The East is Red* the same year, with Joey Wong playing Asia's love interest, leading to some very erotic and ambiguous love scenes which have made it a favourite at gay and lesbian festivals.

Having established this striking and sexually ambiguous screen presence, Brigitte then made *Deadful Melody* (1993) with Yuen Biao, in which she plays a vengeful woman who takes on all comers with a harplike instrument which gives out defeaning soundwaves.

One of her prime cinematic moments came

The Bride With White Hair

Brigitte Lin and Andy Lau relax on the set of The Three Swordsmen

Deadful Melody

Left: Brigitte Lin
gets moody with
Tony Leung in
Dragon Gate Inn

Above:

Deadful Melody

when director Ronnie Yu cast her in the action-meets-arthouse classic *The Bride With White Hair* (1993). She plays the white haired martial arts heroine who captivates the heart and soul of Wu Tang warrior Leslie Cheung and then wreaks horrible revenge. This movie has received wide recognition for its stunning cinematography and powerful screenplay. It is a movie best seen on the big screen. She also starred in the equally attractive but less memorable *The Bride With White Hair 2.*

Brigitte continued her new wave career in Yuen Woo Ping's *Fire Dragon* (1993) and in one of the last big budget new wave films to be lensed, *The Three Swordsmen*, with Andy Lau (1994), in which her role is again sexually ambiguous.

Despite her many love matches (her suitors include Chung Hwa, Charlie Chin, Wang Yu and Jackie Chan) her love life has perhaps been more dramatic than any love story she has portrayed on screen. But recently she retired from the film industry to marry the multi-millionaire businessman who owns the Esprit chain of shops, and gave birth to a daughter. Her last screen performance was in

Wong Kar Wai's superb *Chungking Express*, in which she plays a shady character who picks up a cop in a bar, deals drugs and blows people away without a second thought, adding yet another facet to her repertoire of roles. She had already appeared in his powerful movie *Ashes of Time* in 1993.

A whole book could be written on Brigitte Lin's colourful life and impressive career. She has won many accolades and awards, notably for *Red Dust* (1990) in which she starred alongside Maggie Cheung. In 1991 she even had a TV special dedicated to her. Whether or not she returns to the movie screen, she has had a remarkably long and successful career, spanning over twenty years. Perhaps more than any other actress, she has become an icon of all that is unique and compelling in Hong Kong cinema.

Top: Deadful Melody

Middle: The Bride With White Hair

Middle right: A contemplative Brigitte Lin in Dragon Gate Inn

Bottom right: Brigitte Lin, Tony Leung and Maggie Cheung get mad in Dragon Gate Inn

BRIGITTE-ography

Brigitte Lin / Lin Chin Hsia

1974	Gone With the Cloud
	Ghost in the Mirror
	Moon River
	Girlfriend
	Woman Reporter
	Everywhere Birds are Singing
1975	The Unforgettable Character
	Run Lover Run
1976	Eight Hundred Heroes
	I am Seagull
	Cloud of Romance
	The Chasing Game
	Wonder Sky and Sea
	There's No Place Like Home
	Twenty Tomorrow
	The Typical Admirable Doctor
1977	Dream of the Red Chamber
1978	Love of the White Snake
	A Day on the Beach
1982	Fantasy Mission Force
	The Seven Foxes
	Zu: Warriors From the
	Magic Mountain
1983	All the Wrong Spies
	Be Careful Sweetheart
	Night Orchid
	Black and White
	Demon Fighter
1984	Golden Queen Commando
1985	Pink Force Commando
	Police Story
	Other Side of Gentleman
1986	Dream Lovers
	Peking Opera Blues
	True Colours
1987	The Seventh Curse
	Thirty Million Rush

1987	The Lady in Black
	Flag of Honour
1988	Starry is the Night
1989	Web of Deception
1990	Red Dust
1992	Swordsman 2
	Dragon Gate Inn
	Royal Tramp
	Royal Tramp 2
	Handsome Siblings
	Magnificent Scoundrels
1993	Deadful Melody
	Demi Gods and Semi Devils
	aka The Dragon Chronicles
	The Bride With White Hair
	The Bride With White Hair 2
	Swordsman 3: The East is Red
	Two Eagles
	Shooting Heroes
1993	Black Panther
	Warriors
	Ashes of Time
	Fire Dragon
1994	Three Swordsmen
	Chungking Express

林青霞

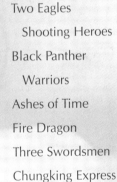

Police Story

Various poses from across the years (top to bottom): 1973, 1975, 1980

ROSAMUND KWAN

關芝琳

"HER SERINE BEAUTY AND STRIKING FEATURES HAS MADE ROSAMUND ONE OF THE SCREEN GODDESSES OF THE NINETIES"

Rosamund Kwan and Donnie Yen are ready to do battle in Tiger Cage 2

rosamund kwan

text:
Rick Baker

Left: Rosamund Kwan is 13th Auntie in Once Upon a Time in China 3

Rosamund
Kwan (Kwan Chi Lam)
was born on September 24,
1963, the only daughter of
Shaw Brothers superstar
Kwan Shan and the equally
famous actress Cheung
Bing Sai. Rosamund
possesses a serene beauty
and her striking features
make her easily
recognisable on screen.
Her family background
brought her into the
entertainment business at
seventeen, when she
became a contract artist for
RTV, which is now known as ATV.

Her career was quickly established and she
was soon placed in dozens of drama projects,
but the hectic workload took its toll. She was
young and an introvert, and these factors
contributed to her premature burn-out. After
only a few years she dropped out of the film
industry. It was during this period that she
married a businessman and ventured into the
fashion business. Sadly, both failed in less
than a year, and she was persuaded to return
to the film set. She has since learned to live in
the limelight.

Rosamund has starred in a number of
successful movies. Her big screen debut was
alongside Chow Yun Fat in *The Headhunter*
(1982) and she went on to star with Jackie
Chan in several of his blockbusters including

Jet Lee and
Rosamund Kwan
in Once Upon a
Time in China

Top: Rosamund Kwan with Jacky Cheung in No More Love, No More Death

Above: Rosamund Kwan kicks ass in Dr Wai in 'The Scriptures With No Words'

Right: Rosamund and Donnie Yen get a surprise in Tiger Cage 2

Twinkle Twinkle Lucky Stars (1985), *Armour of God* (1987) and *Project A part 2* (1987). She also appeared with Samo Hung in *Shanghai Express* (1986) and became a frequent on-screen partner of Andy Lau in movies like *Three Against the World* (1988),

Andy Lau comforts a dying Rosamund Kwan in The Adventurers

A glamourous Rosamund Kwan in The Adventurers

Proud and Confident (1989) and *Casino Raiders* (1989). She was Donnie Yen's love interest in Yuen Woo Ping's classic *Tiger Cage 2* (1990) and also starred with Chow Sing Chi and Andy Lau in *Tricky Brains* (1991). But she is probably most famous for her role as Auntie Yee alongside Jet Lee in the *Once Upon a Time in China* series, and it will not be until these films get a UK release that her fan base here will be as great as she deserves.

More recently, Rosamund has starred in several blockbusters including Ringo Lam's *The Adventurers* (1995) with Andy Lau, and an excellent performance as a good-time girl in *A Touch of Evil* (1995) with Tony Leung

and Michael Wong. Although not a typical action star, she can let rip on screen, as demonstrated in *Doctor Wai in 'The Scriptures With No Words'* (1996) where she shows her lethal skills alongside Jet Lee. Like Anita Mui in *Shanghai, Shanghai,* she attempts some complicated high-wire aerial kicks, flashing a glimpse of thigh in the process! With beauty, brains and talent, she has earned her position as one of Hong Kong's reigning female stars.

Far left:
13th Auntie proudly displays her new possession in Once Upon a Time in China 3
Right:
Rosamund Kwan in Swordsman 2

ROSAMUND-ography
Rosamund Kwan / Kwan Chi Lam

關芝琳

1982	The Headhunter
1984	Challenge on Chasing Girls
	Prince Charming
1985	Twinkle Twinkle Lucky Stars
1986	Shanghai Express
1987	Armour of God
	Project A part 2
1988	Profiles of Pleasure
	Three Against the World
	Vengeance is Mine
	The Crazy Companies 2
	Heart to Hearts
1989	Proud and Confident
	Ghost Fever
	The Last Duel
	Casino Raiders
	I Am Sorry
	What a Small World
198?	The Crazy Companies
1990	Brief Encounter in Shinjuku
	Return to Action
	Tiger Cage 2
	A Bite of Love
	Undeclared War

1991	Tricky Brains	1993	All's Well End's Well, Too
	Inspector Pink Squad		Once Upon a Time in China 3
	This Thing Called Love		No More Love, No More Death
	Once Upon a Time in China	1993	Love Among the Triad
	The Banquet		Blade of Fury
	Alien Wife		The Assassin
1992	Once Upon a Time in China 2	1994	Once Upon a Time in China 4
	The Sting	1995	The Adventurers
	With or Without You		Touch of Evil
	Gameboy Kids	1996	Doctor Wai in
	Swordsman 2		'The Scriptures With No Words'
	Saviour of the Soul 2	?	Pretty Ghost
	Gigolo and Whore 2	?	Mr Smart

cat on a hot tin roof

jade leung

梁琤

text:
Rick Baker

Hong Hong action babe Jade Leung made a dramatic entrance into the world of the femme fatale star in 1991. D&B Films, responsible for showcasing the likes of Michelle Yeoh and Cynthia Khan, were hot to trot in developing more bad girl cinema. The ideal model for them was to be sexy but tough, a woman who knows what she wants and gets it, and with their movie, *Black Cat*, owing some if not all its plotline to Luc Besson's *La Femme Nikita*, the film was guaranteed a high profile in the international market – as was its star. Jade Leung was born in Hong Kong in 1970. As a

Above: Jade Leung takes no shit from a traffic warden in Black Cat
Opposite: Jade in a more tranquil mood

The image that made Jade Leung famous – Black Cat

In an interview with *Eastern Heroes*, we asked Jade why she was picked over so many other beautiful girls. She replied: "I think I had a certain look they wanted, and also I'm very strong. My style was suitable for *Black Cat*."

To be selected was quite an achievement for Jade. In the Hong Kong film industry most performers pay their dues with small roles before becoming stars. Was she nervous before she started shooting? Said Jade: "A little bit, but I liked the character of *Black Cat*, so I felt I could accept the challenge."

Having no previous experience in martial arts, Jade was put through a rigorous training regime to get in shape for the movie. She was taught Chinese kung fu, learned how to react in a fight scene, and also did a lot of weights to tone her body. The film also called for some low key nudity as director Steven Shin had wanted to capitalise on the new found success of the Category III movie. Did Jade find the nude scenes difficult?

"I didn't do the nude scenes deliberately to

young woman she decided to go to Switzerland to continue her education, and stayed there for four years. She learned to speak French and studied fashion design. In 1990 she returned to Hong Kong and it was here, through a friend, that she was introduced to director Steven Shin, who was hunting for a lead for *Black Cat*. Over two hundred girls auditioned for the part, including most of the girls on Hong Kong model agents' books.

classic films it was
Black Cat that pulled
the biggest audience.
The crowds that
gathered in the foyer
were not just the

to shock people or to make my name. They
were part of the script and I knew what to
expect when I accepted the role as I'd been a
model before. I'm not too self-conscious
about my body so I didn't find it too
embarrassing."

Black Cat was to prove a reasonable
success in Hong Kong but has made most of
its money from its international sales and was
recently released in the UK by Made in Hong
Kong. We knew the film would do well on
video here, because a couple of years ago we
were involved in putting a series of Hong
Kong movies together for the NFT for a week-
long festival. Amongst the films were *Eastern
Condors*, *Pedicab Driver*, *The Heroic Trio* and
Drunken Master 2, but despite all these

hardcore kung fu fans who have for so long
supported Hong Kong cinema, but a selection
of City gent types and a fair few of the dirty
mac brigade. I really don't know what they
were expecting as the sex scenes were subtly
shot and tame by comparison to Hollywood
movies – in fact, if *Black Cat* were to come
under any scrutiny here it would be for the
emphasis on violence.

Black Cat not only shot Jade to stardom, but
won her Best Newcomer in Acting at the
Eleventh Hong Kong Film Awards. She was
signed by D&B Films for six films, so it was
no surprise that her follow-up was a sequel,
*Black Cat 2: The Assassination of President
Yeltsin*. Once again she played the
microskirted microchip cutie on the prowl,

JADE-ography
Jade Leung

1991	Black Cat
1992	Black Cat 2
1994	Satin Steel
1995	Green Hat
	Fox Hunter
1996	Enemy Shadow
	Spider Woman

梁珽

Fox Hunter

with Simon Yam, her sidekick in part one, being replaced by Robin Shou (who we all know went on to greater things in *Mortal Kombat*). Although a slightly weaker movie, Jade retained her lethal cocktail of sensuality, vulnerability and icy determination as she blasted the bad guys.

Although D&B subsequently closed up shop, Jade's movie career has continued and she has made several more movies, including *Satin Steel* (1994) alongside rising star Russell Wong, which was more of a fun action comedy with a couple of erotic scenes thrown in for good measure. She also starred in the stagnant *Green Hat* (1995), which was a move away from the action scene for her, and more recently returned to femme fatale mode in *Fox Hunter* (1995). In 1996 she made another action film, *Enemy Shadow*. Jade, always the action woman, insisted on doing her own stunts on this movie, and suffered second and third degree burns when an explosion went badly wrong. They left the scene in the movie (as they tend to do in Hong Kong). Luckily Jade recovered from the incident but her attitude towards doing her own stunts has now changed somewhat and she may use a stunt woman in future productions. Jade has also added another

feature to her CV with *Spider Woman* (1996) with Michael Wong.

Who does Jade admire? Ironically, Julia Roberts, who was almost cast in the American adaptation of *Nikita*, *The Assassin*. She would also, like all Hong Kong actresses, like to be offered the chance to work with Gong Li, or be directed by her former lover Zhang Yimou, and she admires Al Pacino and Martin Scorcese.

Although Jade will forever be recognised for her role in *Black Cat*, she has yet to establish herself as an A-grade actress. But with American directors trolling for good-looking Asian babes, especially those who will do nudity if the script requires it, we may yet see Jade and her contemporaries on the Hollywood circuit.

Jade gets sexy for a pose from Satin Steel

beauty on the beat
joyce godenzi

高麗虹

text:
Rick Baker

Joyce Mina Godenzi (Kao Lai Hung) will be best known to kung fu fans as the beautiful but deadly Vietnamese guerilla fighter who slices her way through the enemy camp in Samo Hung's epic war movie, *Eastern Condors* (1986). In actual fact she is of mixed Chinese and Australian parentage, had no martial arts experience prior to making the movie, and had not even considered a career in the public eye until friends persuaded her to enter the Miss Hong Kong beauty pageant.

Her exotic beauty easily won her the title, and she soon began to get offers of work from film

Joyce Godenzi gets on her bike for
She Shoots Straight

companies. She played the typical girl-next-door role in movies like *The Seventh Curse*, alongside Chow Yun Fat, *Games Gamblers Play*, *Ghost Snatchers* and *Goofy Gang*. But her real break came when Samo Hung cast her against type in the apocalyptic *Eastern Condors*, making movie history and establishing her as a force to be reckoned with.

This fierce bundle of fighting fury with the pretty face and pigtails holds your attention for every frame she appears in as she launches flying kicks and bullets with equal venom, and finally fights to the last blood-splattered moment with one hand amputated by a machete blow. It is an extraordinary performance, but as Joyce revealed in an interview with *Eastern Heroes*, she had no problem with the intensity of the role.

"Samo is the least sexist film-maker in the world," she explained. "He treats women just like men! In the film, my character is clearly a

She Shoots Straight

Licence to Steal

高麗虹

cold-blooded professional soldier, and soldiers sometimes get horribly wounded in battle. If Samo had shied away from that, because I was a woman, then that would have shown disrespect for females."

After this unforgettable role, Joyce took major roles in other movies including Samo Hung's *Spooky, Spooky* (1988), in which she plays a straitlaced cop, a serene foil to the comedic antics of the rest of the cast, and also shows off her Taekwondo skills by kicking off the head of one of the undead. In *She Shoots Straight* (1990) she is again a lady cop, this time taking on gun-toting gangsters rather than walking corpses, and in *Licence to Steal* (1991) she takes on a lady bodybuilder and comes out the victor.

It's hard to believe that she had no martial arts training at all until the making of *Eastern Condors*. In *She Shoots Straight*, directed by Yuen Kwai, who was a classmate of Samo Hung's at Peking Opera School, the full weight of the stunts rested upon her shoulders. She performs high falls, motorbike stunts, fire gags and some incredible acrobatic moves which she had to learn on set. "To begin with the stuntmen put a rope around my waist and then I flip," she recalls. "Then, when I'm confident enough, they take the rope away and I just do the flip by myself. Then, I add the kick on the end. It took me one day to learn,

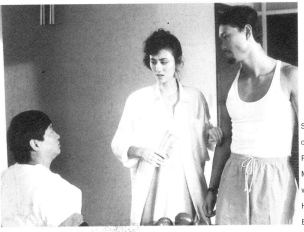
Serious drama in Paper Marriage, with Samo Hung and Billy Chow

working all day and into the night." Add to this the fact that her acting performance is superb, and you begin to see what a terrific asset Joyce Godenzi is to Hong Kong cinema.

Sadly Joyce has not appeared in many movies, and it seems a pity that such a talented actress and impressive screen fighter has not made more of a name for herself. However, Joyce has recently married her mentor and long-time love Samo Hung, so her ties to the movie business remain strong. Let's hope someone persuades this lethal leading lady to return to the screen soon.

She Shoots Straight

MICHIKO NISHIWAKI

Michiko – a rose amongst… men? Hero Dream

西脇美智子

from shy geisha to lethal high-kicking assassin

michiko nishiwaki

Michiko strikes a pose to remember in My Lucky Stars

text: Rick Baker

The first thing I noticed about Michiko Nishiwaki when I met her in the summer of 1990 in London's Chinatown was how slight and petite she was in the flesh compared to the feisty femme fatale action star she plays on screen. It was hard to believe that this Tokyo born actress had won – not once, not twice but three times – the country's bodybuilding championship, and was quite capable of literally sweeping me off my feet, despite my size.

Michiko's first break into film stardom came when Golden Harvest invited her to fly to Hong Kong to play a role in the Jackie Chan blockbuster *My Lucky Stars*. She seemed the ideal choice, as Jackie had a huge fan base in Japan, and the movie was also to be partly set and filmed in Tokyo. Despite her role being

Michiko – the sort of girl you could take home to your mum?

only small, the Japanese audience's familiarity with her would help secure another large box office take for Jackie. In the movie she comes fist to fingernail with fellow action actress Sibelle Hu, dressed in a slinky leotard and with her muscles rippling. It would be hard for anyone who's seen the movie to forget her.

Before invading the Hong Kong movie industry, Michiko was already an established TV star in Japan. She had made numerous appearances on TV and starred in a couple of chanbara Samurai period movies. But Michiko isn't just beauty and brawn. A shrewd businesswoman, she already has several of her own gyms, which she runs with her brother. She makes appearances in soap operas and on talkshows, and is on the panel of judges for the bodybuilding contest in Japan. She believes that these constant public outings will make sure that her name stays in the newspapers.

Despite all this excessive PR in her own country, Michiko still remains something of a

Michiko weaves her magic cat's cradle style in Magic Cop

Hot babe Michiko sizzles on a block of ice in Magic Cop

Dressed to kill or thrill? Michiko in Hero Dream

mystery in Europe, outside of the serious Hong Kong movie followers. This is largely due to the low budget action movies in which she appears, although her face and name are becoming more familiar with the explosion of Hong Kong releases here.

Perhaps her most significant role was opposite Lam Ching Ying in *Magic Cop* (1990), in which she plays the deadly vampire temptress who tries to pit her skills against Mr Vampire himself. She had just completed this movie when I met her. Although her English was poor she tried to communicate through her manager at that time, Kellie Lam, and a demonstration of ghost-busting hand techniques which she called 'natural magic', which she had been taught on set by the maestro, Lam Ching Ying. I understood through the threeway interpretation that she had enjoyed making *Magic Cop* immensely. Her role had been far larger than her previous cameo appearances and she hoped this would lead her to bigger and better things in

the Hong Kong movie industry. However, not only was her English not too good, but she was also struggling to master Cantonese! She believed it was her weird Cantonese accent that had helped secure her the role.

Not withstanding her screen time on *Outlaw Brothers* (1990), where she was really there more as window dressing than anything else, Michiko's biggest break in my opinion was appearing alongside Andy Lau and Chow Yun Fat in the huge hit *God of Gamblers* (1990). In the opening scene she plays the lady gambler who comes off second best against the Do San (Chow Yun Fat). This movie has the unusual distinction of having been released twice and featuring both times in the all-time Japanese box office top ten.

But despite this early career boost, having had her name in the same credits as Jackie Chan, Andy Lau and Chow Yun Fat, Michiko's subsequent selection of film roles has taken her away from the A-grade stardom she seemed to be heading for and has seen her playing second fiddle in many killer B style movies.

If Michiko had really wanted to find instant fame she could have taken another route, because it was at this time in the early nineties that the Category III film was becoming popular. Kellie Lam had said that if the script required it, Michiko was prepared to reveal her body in 'mysterious and erotic ways', whatever that means! I did discover some time afterwards that Michiko had actually posed for a nude photographic session and the photographer wasn't supposed to take shots that were too revealing, but of course, you've guessed it, some did surface in a newspaper later on.

Consequently she was inundated with calls from producers offering her movie roles, and had she pursued this, she could have found herself up there with the Cat III greats like Amy Yip.

However, her career continued to flourish as an action babe, and she made a staggering twenty or so films in less than three years, although most people would be hard pressed to name them. I certainly have yet to discover most of them, as with the low box office take of movies like *The Dragon Fighters* (1989), *Witchcraft Versus Curse* (1990), *Widow Warriors* (1990) and *City Cops* (1990, with

MICH-ography
Michiko Nishiwaki

西脇美智子

1985	My Lucky Stars
	In The Line of Duty 3: Force of the Dragon
1989	The Dragon Fighters
	Princess Madam
1990	God of Gamblers
	Lady Cops
	Outlaw Brothers
	Widow Warriors
	Magic Cop
	City Cops
	The Real Me
	Witchcraft Versus Curse
1992	Avenging Quartet
	Police and Whore
	Hero Dream
1993	Thunder Mission
	Raiders of Lo Sing Treasure

American femme fatale Cynthia Rothrock) her films tend to go straight to video in Hong Kong these days.

None of this seems to daunt Michiko. Financially secure, she can pursue her film roles at leisure, and despite the poor box office performance she finds all her acting roles rewarding. She always puts one hundred percent into her fighting and acting. Asked recently which was her favourite film, she said that she doesn't have one yet but is still hoping that a project will come along which will be a box office success and make people proud of her acting. Once she has done that, she will go back to Japan to concentrate on her business.

For those of you wishing to check Michiko out, we are fortunate enough to have a variety of her movies available on video in the UK, including *My Lucky Stars*, *In The Line Of Duty 3* (released here as *Force of the Dragon*), *Princess Madam*, *Avenging Quartet*, *Widow Warriors*, *City Cops*, *God of Gamblers* and the superb *Outlaw Brothers*. This is a fine selection for anyone wishing to sample the sleek and sexy Michiko. Sadly, none of them have her revealing her body in 'mysterious and erotic ways'. Well, not much.

Michiko and Brigitte Lin

Michiko and Moon Lee on the set of Avenging Quartet

Michiko and Cynthia Khan on the set of Avenging Quartet

Michiko on the other side of the blade

beauty on the screen

cherrie chung

text: Toby Russell

My Darling Genie

Cherrie Chung (Chung Chor Hung) was born in Hong Kong on February 16, 1960. Her big break into the movie scene came while she was working in a toy shop in the infamous Chungking Mansions. She was offered a part in director Johnny To's big screen directional debut, *The Enigmatic Case* (1980), a traditional swordplay flick. He later went on to direct *The Barefoot Kid*.

Cherrie was one of the stunning babes of the eighties. It was her beauty that caught the eye of now-internationally recognised director Ronnie Yu (*The Bride With White Hair*), who cast her opposite the yet-to-be-discovered Chow Yun Fat in Golden Harvest's picture *The Postman Strikes Back* (1981). Chow played an explosives expert and conman, who also does martial arts in this unique kung fu flick.

It was here that Cherrie began her on-screen romance with heart-throb Chow. Director Ann Hui cast them together the same year in *Story of Wu-Viet*. Chow and Cherrie went on to star together in six more great films: *Woman* (1985), *An Autumn's Tale* (1987), *Spiritual Love* (1987), the excellent comedy *The Eighth Happiness* (1988), Ringo Lam's *Wild Search* (1989) and her last movie, John Woo's *Once A Thief* (1991).

鍾楚紅

CHERRIE-ography
Cherrie Chung / Chung Chor Hung

鍾楚紅

1980	The Enigmatic Case
1981	The Postman Strikes Back
	Story of Wu-Viet
1982	Eclipse
	It Takes Two
1983	Hong Kong Hong Kong
	Twinkle Twinkle Lucky Stars
	Winners and Sinners
	The Dead and the Deadly
	Descendants of the Sun
	I Love You Cherrie
1984	My Darling Genie
	Prince Charming
	The Happy Couple
1985	Woman
1986	Spring Outside of the Fence
	Peking Opera Blues
1987	An Autumn's Tale
	Double Fixation
	The Good, the Bad and the Beauty
	One Husband Too Many
	Spiritual Love
1988	Walk On Fire
	The Eighth Happiness
	Moon, Stars and Sun
1989	Wild Search
	Stars and Roses
	Happy Together
198?	Banana Cop
198?	Heaven Can Help
198?	Messenger of Death
198?	Chaos by Design
1991	Zodiac Killers
	Once a Thief
	Yuppie Fantasia
?	Couples, Couples, Couples
?	Goodbye Darling

Cherrie Chung with Chow Yun Fat

Chinese fans wanted Cherrie and Chow to marry because they made such a lovely couple, but in fact there was no off-screen relationship, and Cherrie retired after *Once A Thief* and married a businessman. She was coaxed out of retirement for a TV advert for a watch, produced by her husband.

Once a Thief

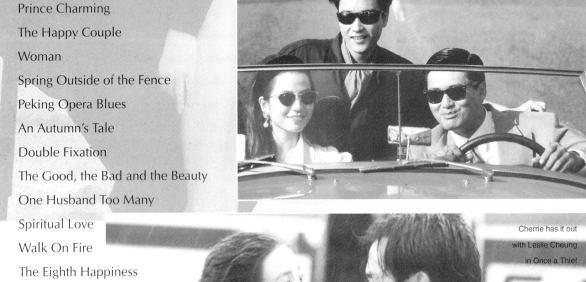

Cherrie has it out with Leslie Cheung in Once a Thief

hollywood hot-shot
joan chen

text:
Rick Baker

Joan Chen (Chen Chung) was born on April 26, 1961 in Shanghai, to parents who came from Zie Zung. She studied English at the Shanghai Foreign Launguage College and upon graduation entered the Shanghai Movie Production Company as a trainee actress. She was spotted by a famous director who cast her in his film *Ching Chun* ('The Youth') as the leading actress, in 1977. For her second film, *Siu Fa Hsiao Hua* ('Little Flower', 1978) she was awarded Best Actress in the Hundred Flowers Awards.

陳沖

She left China in 1981 to study Mass Communication at the University of California. She also did some modelling and studied acting. Her big break came when she landed the key role in *Tai-Pan* (1986) alongside Australian actor Bryan Brown. She then went on to star in the Bertolucci blockbuster *The Last Emperor* (1988) with fellow Chinese actor John Lone.

With the success of this movie Joan became hot property in Hollywood and up until now she is still Tinseltown's leading Oriental lady, giving hope to others pursuing

Salute of the Jugger, one of Joan Chen's non-Asian, English speaking action roles

JOAN-ography
Joan Chen / Chen Chung

1977	Ching Chun
1978	Siu Fa Hsiao Hua
1984	Goodbye My Love
1986	Tai-Pan
1988	The Last Emperor
	Salute of the Jugger
1989	Blood of Heroes
1991	Deadlock/Wedlock
1992	Turtle Beach
1993	Golden Gate
	Temptation of a Monk
1994	Heaven and Earth
	On Deadly Ground
	Red Rose White Rose

陳沖

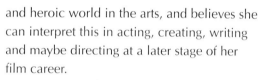

and heroic world in the arts, and believes she can interpret this in acting, creating, writing and maybe directing at a later stage of her film career.

Joan is married to American Chinese producer and acclaimed Wing Chun man Jeff Lau, producer of *Aces Go Places 3* and *Mismatched Couple*, who worked for some time at Cinema City. Now firmly on the Hollywood star list, her film career continues to go from strength to strength, with major roles in Oliver Stone's *Heaven and Earth* (1994) and alongside Steven Seagal in *On Deadly Ground* (1994).

her success. Her international fame brought her back to the Far East, where she worked on projects financed by Hong Kong film companies.

Joan says she is a stubborn person, believing in absolute values and grandiose ideas that derive from her days back in Communist China. She laments that the modern western materialistic world and changing China have long lost the basic, intrinsic values of life. She wants to reproduce her ideal grand

Right:
Joan Chen readies for some brutal action in Salute of the Jugger

a star is born — josephene siu

text:
Rick Baker

Josephene Siu (Siu Fong Fong) was born in Shanghai in 1947. A veteran of the film industry, she started her filming career at the age of seven in a movie called *Tear of Little Star* (1954). From then on, up until 1968, she appeared, incredibly, in nearly 200 movies, and it was in the late sixties and early seventies that she and her contemporary Chan Bo Chu, now retired, dominated the Hong Kong movie scene.

In 1968 she retired to pursue her dream of going back to school and in 1974 she finally achieved her Batchelor degree in Mass Communications at an American university. She returned to the Hong Kong film industry and TV production with great enthusiasm and created the popular comedienne image of Lam Ah Chun. Her divorce from actor Charles Tsun followed soon afterwards.

She re-established herself in the movie industry in the early eighties, starring in movies like *The Spooky Bunch* (1980) and John Woo's *Plain Jane to the Rescue* (1982). She then married Terence Chang, a senior

Josephene Siu instructs Jet Lee on how to carry his swords in Fong Sai Yuk

executive in the Murdoch Group, representing ATV, and they now have two daughters. In 1987 she won Best Actress in the Sixth Hong Kong Film Awards for *The Wrong Couples*.

Her career continued to flourish and in the nineties she starred alongside Chow Sing Chi in *Fist of Fury 1991* and in the sequel, *Fist of Fury 1992*. She also played Jet Lee's mother in *Fong Sai Yuk* 1 and 2 (both 1992). Her recent role in *Summer Snow* (1996) put her back on top, when she was awarded Best Actress in the Golden Awards at the Hong Kong Film Festival. She also won the prestigious Berlin Film Festival award for Best Actress, one of the highest awards a non-Caucasian actress has achieved. The film, which has been awarded much critical acclaim, is currently working its way around the international film festivals, bringing her a new generation of fans.

Like the megastar she is, comparable to Hollywood's Elizabeth Taylor, she has never left the film studio or the bright lights. The noise and the chaotic film scedules have sadly taken their toll on her heath, and she has suffered from tinnitus for most of her life and is almost deaf in one ear. She recently went under anaesthetic to have potentially cancerous cysts removed from her stomach, but her reputation has proved that she is a most strong-willed woman and can endure the most painful things and suffer in silence. When she was admitted to hospital she went in without telling anyone, not even her supportive husband. She explained afterwards that she did not want others, especially her loved ones, to worry.

Her mother, who brought Josephene up single handed, is her biggest fan. Josephene Siu, without doubt, is a remarkable woman with a remarkable career. Her film credits are too many to list exhaustively.

SIU-ography
Josephene Siu /
Siu Fong Fong

1954	Tear of Little Star
1974	Miroshind
	Girlfriend
1976	Jumping Ash
1978	Lam Ah Chun
1979	Lam Ah Chun Blunders Again
1980	The Spooky Bunch
1982	Plain Jane to the Rescue
	The Perfect Match
1984	A Friend From Inner Space
1987	The Wrong Couples
1991	Fist of Fury 1991
1992	Fist of Fury 1992
	Fong Sai Yuk
	Fong Sai Yuk 2
	Legend of the Dragon
1994	Always on My Mind
1996	Summer Snow

蕭芳芳

gong li

Gong Li was born on December 31, 1965, and made her debut in 1988's *Red Sorghum* while she was studying at the Central Drama College in China. She worked for the Drama Laboratory of the college after graduation, before her movie career took off. Since then, she has become the most important and influential Chinese actress of her generation, and the inspiration for the politically controversial films of her former lover, director Zhang Yimou. Gong Li is probably the only Chinese actress to become famous internationally while still working in Chinese movies, and her award-winning films are widely acclaimed on the arthouse circuit, although ironically they are frequently banned in her own country. Her forte is in playing the strong, determined woman struggling against adversity, and it is this boldness which has made her a role model for Chinese women, as well as earning her the reputation for being outspoken, a rare trait in a woman who comes from, and is still grounded in, the oppressive political background of the Mainland. She recently married Singapore businessman Ooi Hoe Seong and is now looking at Hollywood projects.

Gong Li and Leslie Cheung in Tempestuous Moon

Demi Gods and Semi Devils

filmography

1988	Red Sorghum
	Operation Cougar
	The Empress Dowager
1990	A Terracotta Warrior
	Ju Dou
1991	God of Gamblers 3:
	Back to Shanghai
	Raise the Red Lantern
	The Banquet
1992	Story of Qiu Ju
	Mary From Beijing
	Farewell My Concubine
1993	Flirting Scholar
	Demi Gods and Semi Devils
	aka The Dragon Chronicles
1994	The Great Emperor's
	Concubine
	The Great Emperor's
	Concubine 2
	To Live
	La Paintre
1995	Shanghai Triad
1996	Tempestuous Moon

Gong Li and Chow Sing Chi are lost in time in God of Gamblers 3

李嘉欣 michelle reis aka Michelle Lee

Michelle Reis (Lee Kar San) was born on June 20, 1970. Her father is Portuguese and her mother is Chinese. She attended the prestigious Mary Knoll College and matriculated in Saint Paul's College in Hong Kong. In 1988 she was the winner of the Miss Hong Kong beauty pageant and she also won the Miss International Chinatown contest. She then embarked on a career in television, starring in two TV dramas.

Her film debut was *Kau Min Suen Yin* (*The Declaration of Help*, 1990). She then starred with Joey Wong in *A Chinese Ghost Story 2* (1990) and with Andy Lau and Alan Tam in *Casino Raiders: No Risk No Gain* (1990). Her beauty and talent continued to win her constant roles in big production movies including *Swordsman 2* (1991) with Jet Lee, and alongside Chow Sing Chi in *Royal Tramp* 1 and 2 (both 1992). She also worked with femme fatale Cheung Man in Yuen Biao's directorial debut *Kid From Tibet* (1992). In 1993 she starred with Jet Lee again in the classic *Fong Sai Yuk* parts 1 and 2. She is still very active in the Hong Kong film industry.

Sword of Many Loves

Michelle in traditional mode – Zen of Sword

The Wicked City

Michelle is held at gunpoint in The Other Side of the Sea

filmography

1990	The Declaration of Help
	A Chinese Ghost Story 2
	Perfect Girl
	Casino Raiders: No Risk No Gain
1991	Swordsman 2
1992	Wizard's Curse
	Zen of Sword
	Royal Tramp
	Royal Tramp 2
	Kid From Tibet
	The Wicked City
1993	Fong Sai Yuk
	Sword of Many Loves
	Fong Sai Yuk 2
1994	Drunken Master 3
	The Other Side of the Sea
1995	Fallen Angels
1996	July 13th

wu chien lien

吳倩蓮

Wu Chien Lien was born in Taiwan on July 3, 1968. She graduated from the National College of Art in Taipei, majoring in theatrical studies. She frequently participated in stage work while she was still studying, and like many Hong Kong actresses she worked as a model in magazines and advertisements.

She made her film debut alongside Andy Lau in the Director's Guild production *A Moment of Romance* (1990). It was a classic film and a superb performance from Wu Chien Lien which led to a nomination for Best Performer at Hong Kong's Golden Film Awards. Since then her talent has been recognised by the Hong Kong movie industry and she is constantly invited to star in locally produced films. Some of her most acclaimed roles include *Three Summers* (1993), *In Between* (1994), *Treasure Hunt* (1994) and *The Returning* (1994).

International fame came when she landed a role in *Eat Drink Man Woman*, directed by Ang Lee, which depicted the cultural and emotional conflicts of the modern Taiwanese career woman.

She has also, like many Hong Kong stars, made the transition to pop music, and her records sell well in both mainland China and Taiwan. She is romantically close to a childhood friend based in America.

Wu Chien Lien is held captive by Andy Lau in *A Moment of Romance*

Above: Wu Chien Lien gets tied up in *The Adventurers*
Left: Wu with Chow Yun Fat in *Treasure Hunt*

filmography

1990	A Moment of Romance
1991	Casino Raiders 2
1993	Three Summers
	A Moment of Romance 2
	The Barefoot Kid
	The Royal Scoundrel
1994	In Between
	Treasure Hunt
	How Deep is Your Love
	Love and the City
	The Returning
	To Live and Die in Tsim Sha Tsui
	Eat Drink Man Woman
	Beginner's Luck
	Return of God of Gamblers
	Oh My Three Guys
1995	The Adventurers
	Mean Street Story
	Dream Lover
	How Deep is Your Love
1996	A Moment of Romance 3

袁詠儀 anita yuen

Anita Yuen (Yuen Wing Yee) was born in Hong Kong in 1971 and has been one of the discoveries of the nineties. One day she was hosting shows for TVB, the next she was a fully fledged A-grade actress.

Her career took off when she won Best Performer in the Twelfth Hong Kong Film Awards for the send-up movie *The Days of Being Dumb* (1992). She then found mega-stardom when she won Best Actress at the Thirteenth annual awards for her exceptional performance in *C'est La Vie, Mon Cherie* (1993). The following year she won again for *He's a Woman, She's a Man* (1994). Since then she has been one of the most popular comedy actresses in Hong Kong.

Her ambition is to enter into the international film market and she intends to do this by concentrating on fewer projects in 1996, although if Jackie Chan's *Thunderbolt* enjoys the same success as *Rumble in the Bronx* when it opens theatrically in the US this will go some way towards giving her the exposure she is looking for. She has recently been forging relationships with producers and directors who have experience in the international market, and is particularly keen to work with those who have earned a good reputation at the international film festivals.

Although Anita was Miss Hong Kong in 1990, she does not have the traditional look of Chinese beauties. She has more the trendy, punky look popularised by singer Faye Wong, and is happy to play the goofball characters which suit her comic talent.

Anita Yuen, ready to go into action

Bizarre! Whatever You Want

Even more bizarre! The Chinese Feast

From Beijing With Love

filmography

1992	The Days of Being Dumb
	Handsome Siblings
1993	Two of a Kind
	Tom, Dick and Harry
	Legend of the Liquid Sword
	A Warrior's Tragedy
	The Incorruptible
	Sword Stained With Royal Blood
	C'est La Vie, Mon Cherie
1994	It's a Wonderful Life
	I've Got You, Babe
	I Will Wait For You
	Crossings
	Crystal Fortune Run
	He and She
	He's a Woman, She's a Man
	A Taste of Killing and Romance
	Beautician of the Corpses
	The Wrath of Silence
	Tears and Triumph
	From Beijing With Love
	The True Hero
	Whatever You Want
1995	Just Married
	The Chinese Feast
	Thunderbolt
	Mountain Meets Water
	1:00am
	A Fool's Game
1996	Age of Miracles
	Jingle Jingle Lucky Star
	Don't Fool Me
	Hu Du Men
	Tri Star
	Only Fools Fall in Love

carina lau

Lady Supercop

filmography

Carina Lau (Lau Kar-Ling) is a typical Xuzhou beauty, from the province renowned for producing beautiful women in China. She was born there on December 8, 1965, and went to Hong Kong when she was thirteen. She joined TVB's talent training course after high school in 1983 and was fortunate enough to be immediately picked out for an important role in a drama series.

Despite her strong native accent, Carina's classic beauty, coupled with her talent in Chinese musical instruments and acting, ensured a smooth entrance into Hong Kong's entertainment scene. She appeared

Deadful Melody

in many popular TV dramas before breaking into the film industry in 1986. Carina is influenced by the classic Chinese novel *The Red Chamber* and says she has learnt a lot from the mischievous description of the characters and this has helped her understand and express different roles. She compares the world in *The Red Chamber* to the complicated modern world, and says that no matter what time one lives in, being communicative and sociable is the only way to survive.

Her movie career has varied from action films like *China White* (1989) and *Lady Supercop* (1993) to more erotic films like *Profiles of Pleasure* (1988) and *Gigolo and Whore* (1991). She put in a superb performance for Wong Kar Wai in *Days of Being Wild* (1990) and more recently has found box office success playing Chow Sing Chi's wife in *Forbidden City Cop* (1996). She has also recently embarked on

a singing career in Taiwan. More of an actress than an action babe, this talented performer is far more than just a pretty face.

Carina Lau with Maggie Cheung in Project A part 2

1986	Rich and Famous
1987	Tragic Hero
	Project A part 2
1988	Profiles of Pleasure
	Naughty Boys Inc.
	The Romancing Star 2
	City Warriors
	Heart to Hearts
1989	China White
	Lucky Guys
	Return of the Lucky Stars
	I Am Sorry
	Queen's Bench 3
	Four Loves
	She Shoots Straight
1990	Days of Being Wild
	The Banquet
1991	Gigolo and Whore
1992	Girls Without Tomorrow
	Centre Stage
	Rose
	The Night Rider
	Saviour of the Soul 2
	Now You See Love, Now You Don't
	Girls Without Tomorrow
1993	Deadful Melody
	Lady Supercop
	Two Eagles Shooting Heroes
	No More Love No More Death
1994	He's a Woman, She's a Man
	Ashes of Time
1996	Forbidden City Cop

鍾麗緹 christy chung

Christy Chung (Chung Lee Ching) was born and educated in Canada. She graduated from University, majoring in marketing, and was the Champion of the Miss Chinatown of Montreal contest, and the International Miss Chinatown contest in 1993. Holding this title led her straight into the entertainment industry, where she became a contract actress for TVB.

Having grown up in Canada, Christy is easy-going, openminded, adventurous and straightforward, and her friendly personality has made her lots of friends in the sophisticated movie environment. She has also become popular with directors because of her willingness to take her clothes off if the role requires it. She found recognition from the public since starring in a musical programme with singer Aaron Kwok.

Christy's career has developed through the nineties and her popularity keeps growing. She has made films alongside Chow Sing Chi (*Love on Delivery* and *Hail the Judge*, both 1994), and Jet Lee (*Bodyguard From Beijing*, 1994). She recently starred with box office heart-throb Michael Wong in director Wong Jing's *Jingle Jingle Lucky Star*. Apparently her English is better than her Cantonese!

Christy gets to grips with Jet Lee in Bodyguard From Beijing

Simon Yam gets to grips with Christy in Man Wanted

filmography

1993	Perfect Exchange
	The Bride With White Hair 2
1994	Love On Delivery
	Hail the Judge
	Modern Romance
	Bodyguard From Beijing
	Mermaid Got Married
	Whatever You Want
1995	Man Wanted
	Passion '95
	Red Wolf
	High Risk
1996	Tai Chi Master 2
	Jingle Jingle Lucky Star

charlie yeung

楊采妮

Charlie Yeung (Yeung Choi Loi) was born on May 23, 1974 in Taiwan and is the only child of a Shanghainese couple. Shortly after her birth they moved to Hong Kong. She embarked upon her career when she was persuaded to do commercials and modelling while she was still in high school. Her breakthrough came in 1993 when she was cast alongside singing megastar Aaron Kwok Fu Shing in an advert.

She entered the movie industry the same year in the Manga-in-Motion style flick *Future Cops*, and in the following year she starred in Wong Kar Wai's *Ashes of Time*. She also starred in Tsui Hark's *The Lovers* (1994) and the excellent *One Armed Swordsman* remake *What Price Survival?* (1994) alongside David Chiang and Tsui Sui Keung. She has recently embarked upon a singing career.

Above: Charlie poses for the camera

Right: What Price Survival?

filmography

1993	Future Cops
1994	Ashes of Time
	The Lovers
	How Deep is Your Love
	What Price Survival?
1995	Apartment For Women
	Love in the Time of Twilight
	Fallen Angels
	Young Policemen in Love
	How Deep is Your Love
1996	Dr Wai in 'The Scriptures with No Words'

yang hui shan

楊惠珊

The ninja queen of Taiwan started out playing straight swordplay movies and love stories before finding herself cast in a number of ninja pictures, the best being *Challenge of the Lady Ninja*. She currently runs her own business.

filmography

1980	Challenge of the Lady Ninja
	New Blazing Temple
1981	Impossible Woman
	Clan of Righteousness
1982	Island Warriors
	Pink Force Commando
	Golden Queen Commando
	Fantasy Mission Force

Yang Hui Shan goes over the script with director Lee Tso Nam

葉玉卿 veronica yip

Veronica Yip (Yip Yuk Hing, also known as Ronnie Yip) was born in 1967 in Hong Kong. She was the first runner-up in the first Miss Asia Beauty Pageant. She then joined the local television network, ATV, and after six years there made the plunge into the movie industry. Her buxom figure, oozing with sexual chemistry, made her ideal for a career in Category III movies, and she found fame alongside Amy

Bogus Cops

Yip, Pauline Chan and the new wave of nineties adult stars. Her timing was perfect as the Cat III genre was just beginning to get established.

Her debut movie was *Take Me* (1991) and in the same year she completed two more films, *Pretty Woman* and *Hidden Desire*. But Veronica is not just a pretty face and she has been recognised for her acting ability, being nominated at the Thirteenth Hong Kong Film Awards for best actress for *A Roof With A View* and best supporting actress for *Love Among the Triad* (both 1993). She has also, like many other Hong Kong actresses, pursued a career in singing. Veronica is currently active in the film industry and has found many western fans due to her sexy on-screen image, even though there are very few of her movies available on video in the UK. If you want to marvel at this Asian sex goddess, check out *Gigolo and Whore*, in which she co-stars with Simon Yam. She is a must-see for Cat III fans.

filmography

1991	Take Me
	Pretty Woman
	Hidden Desire
1992	Gigolo and Whore
	Cash on Delivery
	Summer Lovers
	Call Girl '92
	Rose
1993	Rose, Rose I Love You
	Three Summers
	Retribution Sight Unseen
	Love Among the Triad
	Hero Beyond the Boundary of Time
	Bogus Cops
	A Roof With A View
	Treasure Island
	Three Days of a Blind Girl
	Man of the Times
	Two Eagles Shooting Heroes
	1941: Hong Kong on Fire
1994	Run
	Red Rose White Rose
	Law on the Brink
	Mermaid Got Married
1995	Scarred Memory
	1:00 am
	Mother of a Different Kind
1996	Hong Kong Iris

BOGUS COPS

走佬威龍

sylvia chang 張艾嘉

Sylvia Chang was born in Taiwan, the daughter of a famous actor, and was a natural choice for Lo Wei when casting for a female lead to play opposite Wang Tao in *Yellow Faced Tiger*. Sylvia is a very competent actress and has even appeared in the US comedy series *M*A*S*H*. She also played opposite Mel Gibson and John Phillip Law in *Attack Force Z* and has directed several pictures including *Sisters of the World Unite*. She won international acclaim as Chi Pore (a lady cop) in the *Aces Go Places* series and in Tsiu Hark's *Shanghai Blues*.

filmography

1975	Chinatown Capers
	Tattooed Dragon
	Yellow Faced Tiger
	Sweet Seventeen
	Hong Kong Superman
	The Story of Four Girls
	Confused Love
	Victory
1976	Posterity and Perplexity
	The Waves
	Love Popcorn
	Dusk of Wild Pigeon
	Erotic Dream of the Red Chamber
	Warmth in Autumn
1976/77	Attack Force Z
1977	Taipei 1977
	Yesterday Dies Too Soon
	The Lady Killer
	Kidnapped
1978	The Golden Age
197?	Crazy Romance
197?	Passion in the Field
197?	Seven Year Itch
197?	That Day on the Beach
1981	Aces Go Places
1982	Aces Go Places 2
1983	Aces Go Places 3
	Red Panther
1984	Shanghai Blues
	He Lives By Night
1986	Aces Go Places 4
	Peking Opera Blues
	Bounty
	Passion
	Immortal Story
1987	Lucky Stars Go Places
	All About Ah Long

1989	Eight Taels of Gold
	Full Moon in New York
	The Fun, the Luck and the Tycoon
1990	My Mother's Tea House
	Queen of Temple Street
1991	Sisters of the World Unite
	A Rascal's Tale
1992	Mary From Beijing
1995	I Want to Live On
	Siao Yu (director)

Sylvia versus Karl Mak
in Aces Go Places

Aces Go Places

利智 nina li chi

Nina Li (Li Chi) was born in Shanghai in 1965. She may well have been destined to end up on the big screen, as her father was an actor too. After graduating from high school she went on to the Shanghai Art University, but dropped out before completing her studies. She moved to Hong Kong in 1981, and also spent time in San Francisco, where she was a student.

Dragon Twins

After enjoying her travels she returned to China, where her voluptuous figure found her some success when she entered several beauty contests. The natural progression from here was to enter the movie industry and like her acting counterparts of that era, Amy Yip and Pauline Chan, the sexual chemistry she exuded and her curvaceous figure found her instant recognition in the industry. She has starred in many classic films, including *Tiger on the Beat* (1988), alongside Chow Yun Fat, where she gets nastily knocked about by Chow while she is covering for her brother, played by Philip Ko, who is a drugs baron. She also starred in the fast-paced Manga-in-Motion flick *Dragon From Russia* (1990) alongside Maggie Cheung, with Samo Hung in the superb action flick *Pedicab Driver* (1989) and with Joey Wong in *A Chinese Ghost Story 3* (1991). She reunited with Maggie Cheung in Jackie Chan's quirky action flick *Dragon Twins* (1992). Her career in more recent times has slowed down but she is still very much in the limelight and is currently the girlfriend of martial arts action superstar Jet Lee – and judging by her pictures, who can blame him!

Dragon Twins

Chow Yun Fat tries to barter with Nina for her handbag in *Tiger on the Beat*

Miracle Ninety Days

Samo and Nina are forever blowing bubbles in Pedicab Driver

filmography

1987	The Criminal Hunter
1988	Tiger on the Beat
	Aces Go Places 5
	The Greatest Lover
1989	Pedicab Driver
	Dragon Fight
	What A Small World
	Four Loves
	Profiles of Pleasure
	Seven Year Itch
1990	Dragon From Russia
	To Spy With Love
	Perfect Girls
	The Spooky Family
1991	The Fun, the Luck and the Tycoon
	Legend of the Chiu Chow Brothers
	Inspector Pink Dragon
	Stone Age Warriors
	A Chinese Ghost Story 3
1992	Miracle Ninety Days
	Lover's Tear
	Dragon Twins
	Kid From Tibet

nina li chi

利智

Legend of the Chiu Chow Brothers

faye wong

王靖雯

Chungking Express

Faye Wong in concert

Chungking Express

Faye Wong is the current queen of Canto Pop, and it was a great coup for director Wong Kar Wai to lure her onto the screen for the critically acclaimed *Chungking Express* (1995).

Faye was born on August 8, 1969 in Beijing, and was one of the first generation of pop singers in capitalist China. She moved to Hong Kong in 1990 and signed to TVB. After working hard on her Cantonese she landed several popular roles in TV dramas, as well as becoming a singing superstar. Her controversial, punky image has made her the subject of much gossip and she is a pop icon for Hong Kong teenagers. She is said to be heavily influenced by Irish pop band The Cranberries and has recently commissioned British band The Cocteau Twins to write songs for her.

Faye was nominated for the Best Actress award for her quirky role in *Chungking Express*, in which she gives a superb performance as the gawky, Mamas and Papas-obsessed girl who sneaks into an apartment in Chungking Mansions to erase traces of her rival for a melancholy cop's attention. Since then she has been inundated with script offers, and it is to be hoped she will return to the screen soon.

葉童 cecilia yip

Cecilia Yip (Yip Tung – no relation to Amy Yip!) was born on March 8, 1962. She launched her career as a model in 1980 and entered the film industry in 1982 when she was spotted by director Patrick Tam (*The Sword*) in a cinema queueing for tickets and invited to feature in his movie *Nomad*, which also starred a young Leslie Cheung. She then landed the lead role in the excellent, underrated gangster feature *Coolie Killer*, alongside Hong Kong heart-throb Charlie Chin, for which she won a Golden Award for the best new talent in Hong Kong films.

Her accolades have continued to mount up – she won Best Actress for *Let's Make Laugh* in 1984, for *Beyond the*

It's bathtime for Cecilia in The Swordsman

Love, Guns and Glass

filmography

1982	Nomad
	Coolie Killer
1983	Let's Make Laugh
	Esprit d'Amour
1984	Hong Kong 1941
1985	Infatuation
1986	Strange Bedfellows
	Last Song in Paris
	My Heavenly Lover
1987	Reincarnation
	Wonder Woman
	Amnesty Decree
1988	Chaos by Design
	Carry On Hotel
	Fumbling Cops
	Set Me Free
1989	Beyond the Sunset
1990	The Swordsman
	Rebel From China
1991	Weakness of Man
	This Thing Called Love
	To Be Number One
1992	Girls Without Tomorrow
1993	Lord of the South China Sea 2
	Crazy Hong Kong
	The Final Judgement
1994	Organized Crime and Triad Bureau
	King of the Sea
	Right Here Waiting
	1941: Hong Kong On Fire
1995	Peace Hotel
	Love, Guns and Glass
?	Those Were the Days
?	Those Were the Days 2

Sunset in 1990, and for *This Thing Called Love* in 1992. She has had a strong film career and like many Hong Kong actresses has attracted many fans, which bemuses her, as she publically claims she has a 'plain face', and is a very private person but loves acting dearly. Unlike some actresses, she believes the only way to keep herself in the industry is to establish herself as a serious actress, like Hollywood's Meryl Streep. Again, sadly, very few of her films have found their way to the UK, but it is possible that films like *The Swordsman* (1990), *To Be Number One* (1991) and *Organized Crime and Triad Bureau* (1994) will one day get a release in the UK. More recently she acted alongside Chow Yun Fat in his farewell Hong Kong film *Peace Hotel* (1995), where she wooed her way into his life by pretending to be his trouble and strife! Cecilia is married to Hong Kong film producer Chan Kwok He.

A moment of angst for Cecilia and Simon Yam in Love, Guns and Glass

vivienne chow

周慧敏

Vivienne Chow (Chow Hai Mee) is a vivacious actress who was born on December 6, 1966 in Hong Kong. Her father recognised her beauty at an early age and nominated her for the Miss Hong Kong competition in 1985, after she finished high school. Although she did not win the beauty pageant her looks and charisma attracted the interest of TVB and she was invited to join as an artist in the drama department, where she enjoyed a succesful career until 1994.

During this time she also was carving out a name for herself in the film industry although she has not enjoyed the same plaudits as in her TV career. Her popularity soon flourished in Japan and her Sino-Japanese TV series has been one of the biggest blockbusters of recent years. She is an enigmatic figure in the highly materialistic Hong Kong entertainment scene, and has a great interest in the I Ching and Zen Buddhism.

Although not really an action babe, she did appear in the fast paced martial art flick *Fun and Fury* (1992) and in the new wave movie *The Kung Fu Scholar* (1994). Her career is still very active, although she has yet to get the acknowledgement she deserves in the UK due to the lack of availability of her movies on video.

Vivienne Chow –
She'll steal your heart

Unmatchable Match, with Chow Sing Chi and Chan Wai Man

filmography

1988	Heart to Hearts
1989	Pelle the Conqueror
	Happy Together
	Romancing the Star 3
1990	Goodbye
	Unmatchable Match
1991	The Perfect Match
	Devil's Vendetta
	Fruit Punch
	Angel Hunter
1992	Arrest the Restless
	Fun and Fury
	Girls Without Tomorrow
1994	Modern Callgirls
	The Kung Fu Scholar
	To Love Ferrari
1996	Top Banana Club

It's a kind of magic... mirror. Mr Vampire 4

loletta lee

Despite the heavy competition from femme fatale beauties adorning the pages of this book, Loletta Lee (Lee Lai Chun) has been named the sexiest woman in Hong Kong – and that's official. This poll wasn't drawn up from western admirers, but in a recent magazine survey in Hong Kong she was said to be the most sexually desired woman among young men. This sexual appeal probably stems from a string of sexy roles she has played in recent years.

She was born on January 8, 1966 and is a native Cantonese. She finished high school at 18 and immediately entered the film industry. Her break came when she was offered the chance to appear in *Everlasting Love* (1984), directed by Johnny Mak (*Long Arm of the Law*). From then on her career spiralled into a huge filmography. Amongst her films, she was most recognised for her role in *My Family* (1986), a blockbuster which broke all box office records at that time. Was it a good film? Not having seen it, I can only speculate as to whether its success was due to a good story or simply the appeal of Loletta's gorgeous face and figure. She also starred in the highly successful *It's a Mad Mad Mad World* trilogy, and set temperatures rising in the superb *Hot Hot and Pom Pom*, (aka *Hong Kong Lethal Weapon*, *Hard Boiled Killers*, 1992) alongside another screen vamp, Bonnie Fu. Enough femme fatale flesh to make any fan's heart flutter!

Her career is still active and she has made so many films it would be impossible to list them all. It is worth noting that her excellent performance won her a nomination for best actress in the Hong Kong Film Awards in 1988 for her role in *Final Victory*. She is another femme fatale who hasn't found much recognition in the west due to the lack of available videos. I suggest you go out and pester your local video company.

李麗珍

filmography

1984	Everlasting Love
	Before Dawn
	The Happy Ghost
	Shanghai Blues
1985	Merry Christmas
	For Your Heart Only
	Crazy Games
	The Flying Mr. B
	The Isle of Fantasy
1986	Kiss Me Goodbye
	My Family
	Devoted to You
1987	You're Okay, I'm Okay
	Porky Meatballs
	It's a Mad Mad Mad World
	Final Victory
1988	It's a Mad Mad Mad World 2
	Bless This House
	Keep on Dancing
	Mr Vampire 4
1989	It's a Mad Mad Mad World 3
	The Wild Ones
	Running Hate
	Jail House Eros
	aka Jail House Girls
1990	Chicken a la Queen
	The Heartbreak Yakuza
	Off Track
	Goodbye Hero
	Saga of the Phoenix
1991	Shanghai 1920
	Off Track
1992	Gun 'N' Rose
	Musical Vampire
	Hot Hot and Pom Pom
1993	Crazy Love
	The Spirit of Love
1994	Girls Unbutton

teresa mo

There is little known about this Hong Kong actress, and yet I dare say most people who are reading this book will have seen her. She has starred alongside Andy Lau in *Don't Fool Me* (1991), with Chow Sing Chi and Amy Yip in *Magnificent Scoundrels* (1991), she also made another film in the same year with Chow Sing Chi, playing the henpecking sister in *Legend of the Dragon*, and she co-starred with Carina Lau in *Lady Supercop* (1993). But she is best known as Chow Yun Fat's ex-girlfriend in John Woo's *Hard Boiled*.

毛舜筠

filmography

1991	Don't Fool Me	1992	My Americanized Wife
	Daddy, Father, Papa		Hard Boiled
	Her Fatal Ways		All's Well That Ends Well
	Mainland Dundee		Now You See Love, Now You Don't
	Magnificent Scoundrels	1993	Lady Supercop
	Red Shield		Laughter of the Water Margin
	Legend of the Dragon		All's Well That Ends Well Too
1992	'92 Legendary La Rose Noir		Perfect Couples

Top: Teresa Mo with Chow Sing Chi in Legend of the Dragon

Above: As Chow Yun Fat's ex- in Hard Boiled

sandy lam

林憶蓮

Sandy Lam joined commercial radio in 1982 as a part time disc jockey. In 1984 she joined Sony Records Company Ltd and issued her first album the next year. Her film career began in 1985 when she was cast alongside Leslie Cheung in the film *The Intellectual Trio*. Despite the reasonable success her films have achieved, including a fighting femme role alongside Andy Lau and Rosamund Kwan in *Three Against the World* (1988), she has devoted most of her efforts to becoming a successful singer. She has achieved platinum sales with her albums and has won a string of awards for her singing.

filmography

1985	The Intellectual Trio
1986	Who's the Crook
1988	Keep on Dancing
1988	The Haunted Cop Shop 2
1988	Three Against the World
1990	Shanghai Shanghai

Above: Three Against the World

吳君如 sandra ng

The new look Sandra Ng

Another Hong Kong actress who has a huge filmography but has failed to attract any attention in the western market, Sandra is renowned for playing the comedic foil to movie beauties, and is often the butt of jokes. However, recent makeover shots suggest that there is another side to Sandra, and there may well be a fully-fledged Asian babe waiting to be discovered beneath her comedienne image, although it would seem that producers and directors are happy to keep typecasting her. Indeed, when she changed her image and lost some weight, the acting work seemed to dry up! The industry always needs character actresses to support the more glamorous starlets, but let's hope Sandra gets her chance to shine someday.

filmography

1988	Thunder Cops
	aka Operation Pink Squad
	The Inspector Wears a Skirt
1989	Thunder Cops 2
	aka Operation Pink Squad 2
	Crocodile Hunters
	They Came to Rob Hong Kong
	Ghost Busting
	Vampire Versus Vampire
1990	Vampire Settle on Police Camp
	Ghostly Vixen
	Mortuary Blues
	Raid on Royal Casino Marine
	Love is Love
	Here Comes a Vampire
	When Fortune Smiles
	All For the Winner
	Fire Phoenix
	The Inspector Wears a Skirt 2
1991	Return of the Evil Fox
	The Top Bet
	Money Maker
	Vampire Kids
1992	The Inspector Wears a Skirt 3
	King of Beggars
	Changing Partners
	All's Well That Ends Well
	Miracle 90 Days
	True Love
	Royal Tramp
	Royal Tramp 2
	Cash on Delivery
	Forced Nightmare
	Gameboy Kids
	Sisters in Law

1993	Vampire Family
	All's Well That Ends Well Too
	Perfect Couples
	The Eight Hilarious Gods
	Holy Weapon aka Seven Maidens
	The Inspector Wears a Skirt 4
1994	Always be the Winners
	I Will Wait For You
	Her Fatal Ways 4
	Fire Dragon
	Modern Romance
	The Returning

lee yuen wah

李啟華

Little known Hong Kong actress who found fame on the big screen in *Satin Steel* alongside Jade Leung after appearing in a string of TV dramas and potboiler movie roles. An actress who is not afraid to show the odd gusset shot!

Gusset shots aplenty in Satin Steel

cheung man

張敏

Cheung Man and Chow Sing Chi in King of Beggars

This hard-hitting femme fatale from Mainland China has a huge filmography. Despite her athletic figure and Purdy-style haircut she has yet to gain any real recognition in the UK, although this very cute actress will, when the exposure comes, develop an army of fans. She has put in many notable performances, including *The Swordsman*, with Sam Hui, the unofficial sequel to *God of Gamblers*, with Andy Lau and Chow Sing Chi, the lovely but deadly spider woman in *Holy Weapon* and in *Kung Fu Cult Master*, alongside Jet Lee. She hovered to perfection alongside Brigitte Lin and Gong Li in the frantic fast-paced fantasy flick *The Dragon Chronicles*, also known as *Demi Gods and Semi Devils*. Her mainstay of blockbusters has been appearing in many of Chow Sing Chi's films, including the *Fight Back To School* trilogy, *King of Beggars* and *Hail the Judge*. I'm sure there's a whole chapter on this Chinese bundle of fury, but

for now you'll have to make do with checking out her extensive filmography and forming your own opinion. She gets my thumbs up.

Demi Gods and Semi Devils

filmography

1985	The Magic Crystal
1989	Romancing the Star 3
1990	Story of Kennedy Town
	The Swordsman
	My Neighbours are Phantoms
	God of Gamblers 2
	All For the Winner
	Dragon Killer
1991	Tiger Cage 3
	Devil's Vendetta
	The Fatal Game
	Fight Back to School
	A Chinese Legend
	Fist of Fury 1991
	Lee Rock
	Lee Rock 2
	Dance with the Dragon
1992	Call Girl '92
	Deadly Dream Woman
	Rhythm of Destiny
	King of Beggars
	It's Now or Never
	To Miss with Love
	Fight Back to School 2
	Truant Heroes
	Royal Tramp
	Handsome Siblings
	Fist of Fury 1992
	Invincible
	Cheetah on Fire
1993	Holy Weapon aka Seven Maidens
	The Sword of Many Loves
	Kung Fu Cult Master
	Flying Daggers
	Legend of the Liquid Sword
	Fight Back to School 3
1994	Underground Judgement
	Demi Gods and Semi Devils aka The Dragon Chronicles
	Hail the Judge
	Crystal Fortune Run
1995	Romantic Dream
1996	Ten Brothers
199?	School Commandos

Holy Weapon, aka Seven Maidens

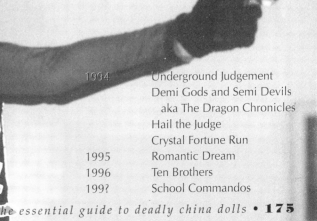

Deadly Dream Woman

yu li

于莉

You'll know the movies even if you don't know the actress. She's appeared alongside Samo Hung in *My Flying Wife* (1991), with Chow Yun Fat in *Prison on Fire 2* (1991), with Simon Yam in the very under-rated Category III classic *A Day Without Policemen* and more recently in the new wave swordplay flick *The Three Swordmen*.

Yu Li and Simon Yam at the ready in A Day Without Policemen

Daughter of Darkness

filmography

1991	My Flying Wife
	Prison on Fire 2
	Hong Kong Godfather
1993	The Trail
	A Day Without Policemen
	Daughter of Darkness
1994	The Three Swordsmen
1995	Xiu Xiu

lilly chung

鍾淑慧

Lilly Chung was the champion in the Miss Hong Kong Universal Beauty Pageant. After that she joined the local television network TVB. It was there that she hosted a series of TV programmes and also found herself cast in some of the soap opera dramas, but when her contract was terminated in Sepetember 1993 she gained mediocre success as an actress in adult movies. Her most famous performances include *Daughter of Darkness* (1993), *Brother of Darkness* (1993), *Fatal Encounter* and in the sick and twisted *Red To Kill* (1994). She also took a predominant role as an action femme fatale in the nothing-to-do-with-Bruce-Willis production *Die Harder* (1995).

filmography

		1994	Fatal Encounter
1993	Daughter of Darkness		Fatal Obsession
	Brother of Darkness		Red To Kill
1994	The Modern Love	1995	Die Harder

Die Harder

cathy chow

周海媚

Cathy Chow was born on 6th December 1966. Her beauty took a natural course and she participated in the Miss Hong Kong Beauty Pageant in 1985. This led her to a contract with TVB where she remained from 1986 to 1994. She most recently starred in Samo Hung's comeback film *Don't Give a Damn!* (1995).

Don't Give a Damn!

irene wan

Irene Wan (Bic Ha) was born in Hong Kong on 30th July 1966 and she made her very first screen appearance in the film *Lonely 15* when she was, coinciden-tally, only 15. She went on to star and co-star in approximately 15 films between 1982 and '89 and is still active in today's film industry. She apparently reveals all in her new movie alongside Simon Yam, called *All of a Sudden*. Her other notable performances are in *Lai Shi, China's Last Eunuch* and alongside Anita Mui and Alex Man in the classic film *Rouge*, which has been on UK television and is also available in the UK on video.

Circus Kids

The Lap of God

溫碧霞

filmography

1982	Lonely 15
	Happy 16
1983	Possessed
	The Sensational Pair
	The First Time
1984	Everlasting Love
	Pom Pom
1986	Love Unto Waste
	Caper
1988	Rouge
	Lai Shi, China's Last Eunuch
	Tiger Cage
1988	Ruthless Family
1989	Bloody Brotherhood
	Hearts No Flowers
	Running Mate
	Armageddon
	The Wild Ones
1990	Fatal Vacation
	The Sniping
	The Tigers
1991	Touch and Go
	The Lap of God
1994	Mr Sardine
	Circus Kids
1996	All of a Sudden

gloria yip

This actress is best known for portraying young characters due to her child-like features. Particular films of note include *Saviour of the Soul*, in which she is a twenty-something actress playing a very innocent young schoolgirl. She could even be termed as jail-bait if you haven't seen her birth certificate. She also starred in the *Peacock King* sequel *Saga of the Phoenix*.

葉蘊儀

filmography

1989	The Peacock King
1990	Demoness From One Thousand Years
	Saga of the Phoenix
	Promising Miss Bowie
1991	Saviour of the Soul
	Blue Jean Monster
	Rebel From China
1992	The Cat
	Misty
1993	Flying Daggers
	Two Eagles Shooting Heroes

do do cheng

鄭裕玲

Carol Cheng (Cheng Yu Ling) was born on Spetember 9, 1957 in Hong Kong. She is more familiarly known as Do Do Cheng. In Szechuanese dialect Do Do means 'fat fat', and this was a nickname given to her as a young girl, as she was plump. Despite that she has flourished into a lean, durable actress. Her father, Sai Gwa Pao, was a veteran actor, making over two hundred movies. He was best known for playing Wong Fei Hung's assistant in the early black and white movies, and can also be seen in films like *Young Master* and *Magnificent Butcher*.

Do Do entered the entertainment industry in 1975 when she joined up with RTV (now ATV), appearing in many TV soap operas. Later she switched to the opposition, TVB, to further develop her career. She made her film debut in 1983 in *The Last Affair*. She won Best Debutante in the following year's Hong Kong Film Awards for that performance. Since then she has starred in dozens of movies, indeed too many to track down. She will be most familiar to the British audience for co-starring alongside Jackie Chan in *Armour of God 2: Operation Condor* (1991). She has won much critical acclaim and several awards including Best Actress in the 25th Golden Horse Awards for *Moon, Star, Sun* (1986) and Best Actress for *Her Fatal Ways* (1990), which produced three sequels. She is more a character actress than a glamour babe.

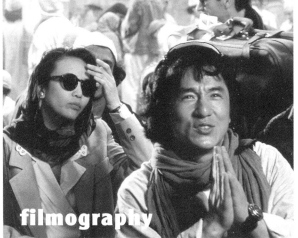

filmography

Carol Cheng, aka Do Do, with Jackie Chan in Armour of God 2

1983	The Last Affair
1986	Moon, Star, Sun
	You Will, I Will
1987	Sister Cupid
	The Romancing Star
	Wonder Woman
	Mr Handsome
1988	No Vampire
	Ghost in the House
	Mr Possessed
	Tiger Cage
	Women's Prison
	Heart to Hearts
	Law or Justice
	The Eighth Happiness
	The Crazy Companies 2
1989	All Night Long
	Perfect Match
	Doubles Cause Troubles
	Burning Sensation
	The Yuppie Fantasia
	The Nobles
	Gift From Heaven
1990	Heart into Hearts 2
	Brief Encounter in Shinjuku
	Promising Miss Bowie
	Her Fatal Ways
	Queen's Bench 2
	The Other Half
1991	Armour of God 2: Operation Condor
	The Top Bet
	Her Fatal Ways 2
	To Catch a Thief
	Slickers Vs Killers
	The Banquet
1992	Never Ending Summer
	Heart Against Hearts
	Once a Black Sheep
	Her Fatal Ways 3
	Second to None
	She Starts the Fire
	Holy Weapon aka Seven Maidens
1994	Her Fatal Ways 4
	It's a Wonderful Life

Once a Black Sheep

Do Do gets down to some serious scrubbing in Holy Weapon

elizabeth lee

李美鳳

A **sultry** Singaporean actress who can make temperatures rise. She has had some minor exposure in the UK through the video releases of *Return Engagement* and *Widow Warriors*, but the piece de resistance for her was appearing opposite Anthony Wong in *Love To Kill*. How much sexual abuse can one woman take? Although sadly it will never see the light of day in England officially, people living elsewhere in the world should check this Category III classic out.

Elizabeth Lee and Alex Man in
He Who Chases After the Wind

Portrait of a Nymph
Portrait of a Nymph
Return Engagement

filmography

1985	Above the Law
1988	Portrait of a Nymph
	Web of Deception
1989	How to be a Millionaire
	All Night Long
	Gunmen
	Long Arm of the Law 3
	Blonde Fury
	City Squeeze
	Yuppie Fantasia
1990	Return Engagement
	Widow Warriors
	Rain, Sunshine, Friends
	He Who Chases After the Wind
1991	Mission of Condor
	Deadly Deal
1992	Freedom Run
1993	Love to Kill
	Sword Stained With Royal Blood
1994	Organised Crime and Triad Investigation Bureau
1995	A Touch of Evil

chow kar ling

周嘉玲

C **how Kar Ling** is a graduate of the University of Hong Kong and was runner-up in the Miss Hong Kong Beauty Pageant in 1991. She has appeared in several films, including some of an adult nature like *Twenty Something* and *Lover of the Last Empress* and more recently as the high flying air stewardess and ex-girlfriend of Tony Leung in Wong Kar Wai's *Chungking Express*.

filmography

1993	He Ain't Heavy He's My Father
1994	Twenty Something
	Chungking Express
1995	Dream Killer
	Lover of the Last Empress
	Ghostly Bus

Chungking Express

羅慧娟 law wai kuen

Law Wai Kuen, also known as Jaqueline Law, is another actress who has yet to make any impact on western audiences. I first noticed her when I saw her Jade Leung-like figure brandishing a bottle for a movie entitled *Ms Butterfly* (1992). Sadly the film did not live up to the expectations of this very sellable visual. She also starred alongside Carrie Ng in the excellent *Remains of a Woman* (1993).

filmography

1992	Mad Mad Ghost
1993	Co-Habitation
	Remains of a Woman
	Ms Butterfly
1994	Switchover
	True Hero

Law Wai Kuen feels a little tyred in Ms Butterfly

吳雪雯 ng suet man

Ng Suet Man aka Jacqueline Ng will set temperatures rising when the eagerly awaited, unofficial sequel to *Naked Killer* – *Raped by an Angel* – gets its UK release. Once again the publicity campaign for this film worked wonders in Hong Kong. Like the campaign for *Naked Killer* featuring Carrie Ng and Chingamy Yau, Jacqueline, who replaces Carrie Ng on the film posters, will certainly have men wearing bibs to catch the dribble. In the movie she portrays a pin-up girl who has to put up with the perverted innuendos from actor Mark Cheng. The film caused some controversy on its release in Hong Kong and some people found the posters obscene which caused several of them to be outlawed. I presume we will have the same reaction in the UK if we stick the girls up next to a Wonderbra poster. Jacqueline is still active in Hong Kong cinema and more recently starred alongside box office megastar Jet Lee in *Kung Fu Cult Master* (1994) and *New Legend of Shaolin* (1994).

filmography

1990	Against All
1991	Running on Empty
1993	Hero Beyond the Boundary of Time
	An Emotional Girl's Doubt of Undress
	Raped by an Angel aka Naked Killer 2
1994	Baron of Gamblers
	New Legend of Shaolin
	Kung Fu Cult Hero

Raped by an Angel

Jacqueline Ng gets the couch treatment in Raped by an Angel

pauline wong

王小鳳

Pauline Wong was born in Canada in 1962. She had her first movie break when she appeared in David Lai's horror flick *Possessed* in 1983. She went on to star in *Possessed 2* (1984) and in the cult Argento-style slasher flick *Night Caller* (1985). Later that year she played the lead role in *Love With the Perfect Stranger*, which earned her Best Actress in the Fifth Hong Kong Awards. Between 1983 and 1990 she starred and co-starred in more than twenty films, including *Mr Vampire* (1985), the Chow Yun Fat double header *Rich and Famous* and *Tragic Hero* (1987), Johnny Mak's powerful *Long Arm of the Law 2* (1987), in the babe-laden film *Profiles of Pleasure* (1988) and alongside Yuen Biao in the excellent fantasy *The Peacock King* (1989). More recently she has gone behind the camera and was an executive producer on *Right Here Waiting* (1994), in which she also starred.

Mr Vampire gets another fan...

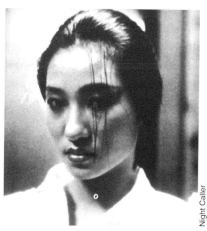

Night Caller

filmography

1983	Possessed
1984	Possessed 2
1985	Night Caller
	Love With the Perfect Stranger
	Mr Vampire
1986	Missed Date
	New Mr Vampire
	Lucky Stars Go Places
	The Story of Dr Sun Yat Sen
1987	Tragic Hero
	Split of the Spirit
	Rich and Famous
	Spiritual Love
	Double Fixation
	Long Arm of the Law 2
	New Mr Vampire 2
1988	No Compromise
	Lai Shi, China's Last Eunuch
	Her Vengeance
	Profiles of Pleasure
	The Greatest Lover
	Web of Deception
1989	The Peacock King
	Four Loves
1990	The Spooky Family
1991	Don Huang Tales of the Night
	The Blue Jean Monster
	Spiritual Trinity
1993	Lover of the Swindler
1994	Right Here Waiting (exec prod)

pang dang

彭丹

Pang Dang, an up-and-coming Category III starlet who intends to carve a career in films of a less erotic nature, has started to make waves in Hong Kong. She already has several films under her skin-tight belt including her latest starring role in *Midnight Caller*. Brought up in the Mainland, she also spent some time in the United States where she studied ballet. Whether her career follows that of Chingamy Yau into action productions or she ends up in straight-to-video soft core erotic movies, without a doubt Pang Dang has got the looks to raise any self-respecting femme fatale fan's temperature.

Another Wonderbra busting shot of Pang Dang

amy kwok

郭藹明

Amy Kwok was the champion in the Miss Hong Kong Beauty Pageant in 1991. Since then she has appeared in numerous TV programmes organised by TVB and in 1993 ventured into movies when she appeared in Jet Lee's martial arts epic *Fong Sai Yuk 2* (1993).

tien niu

恬妞

Tien Niu was born in 1958 in Shanghai. At the age of eight she participated in the Peking Opera, which served to enhance the ability of any kung fu actor or actress. Her debut film was *The Child in Red*, and when she was only sixteen she played the lead in a film entitled *Early Marriage* (1974). She has starred and co-starred in more than sixty films in Taiwan and Hong Kong between 1968 and 1989. She then began to carve out a career in singing and on the stage, and since her retirement from movies in 1989 she has concentrated on these two professions. She was formerly married to Heroic Bloodshed star Alex Man.

Just Heroes

filmography

?	The Child in Red
1974	Early Marriage
1975	Sweet Seventeen
	A Happy Affair
1977	Laugh, Laugh, Laugh
	The Brotherhood
1978	Young Lovers
	Eternal Love
1979	Love is Forever
1980	Lackey and the Lady Tiger
1985	Funny Face
1988	The Other Half and the Other Half
	Gangland Odyssey
	City War
1989	Unfaithfully Yours
	Just Heroes
	Little Cop
	Widow Warriors
	The Trail

bo bo fung

馮寶寶

filmography

1966	Sword and the Lute
	Twin Swords
	Red Lotus Temple
1990	Hong Kong Gigolo
1992	'92 Legendary Rose Noir
	Girls Without Tomorrow
1993	Yes To You, Yes To Me, Yesterday
1994	C'est La Vie Mon Cherie
	It's a Wonderful Life
	Right Here Waiting
1995	Fake Emperor
	Mother of a Different Kind

An aclaimed actress began acting at the age of six. She is the sister of screen villain Fong Hak On. She also spent three years in London window dressing. In recent years she has won several awards for adult roles including Best Supporting Actress in the 1992 Hong Kong Film Awards for *'92 Legendary Rose Noir* and in 1994 for *C'est La Vie Mon Cherie*. She first came to attention alongside Simon Yam in the Category III film *Hong Kong Gigolo*.

tsui ho ying

徐濠縈

After completing her secondary education, Tsui Ho Ying took a secretarial training course, then joined a model agency. She was cast in singing superstar Andy Lau's video for his hit *Thank You For Your Love*. She then became a contract actress with the movie company Team Work Productions.

filmography

1993	Days of Tomorrow
1994	Wonder Seven
1994	The Crucifixion
1994	Victory
1995	Dr. Mack

deannie ip

葉德嫻

An actress from the eighties whose first media break was on Hong Kong television. She later went on to be Samo Hung's love interest in *Dragons Forever* and also starred in *Phantom Bride* (1987).

filmography

1987	Dragons Forever
	Spiritual Love
	Phantom Bride
	Fantasy Romance
1991	Dance With Dragon
1992	Deadly Dream Woman
?	A Time to Die

Deadly Dream Woman

jennifer chan

Jennifer Chan opened a photo shop in Taiwan, and thanks to her initiative in putting pictures of herself in the window (albeit somewhat vain) she was discovered by a well-known director. As a result this started her career as a singer and actress. She has some recognition in the UK due to the Channel 4 screening of *Rock 'N' Roll Cop*.

filmography

1993	Thou Shalt Not Swear
	Black Panther Warriors
1994	Rock 'N' Roll Cop

Rock 'N' Roll Cop

陳明眞

monica chan

Hong Kong actress, little known about, who has starred in *Perfect Girl* (1990) and the unofficial sequel to *God of Gamblers*, *God of Gamblers 2*, starring Andy Lau and Chow Sing Chi (1990). She also appeared in *Casino Raiders 2: No Risk No Gain*.

crystal kwok

郭錦恩

Born on 13th May 1966, Crystal Kwok won the Miss Chinatown contest while she was still in school and will be best remembered by western audiences for her role alongside Jackie Chan in *Dragons Forever* as the young bespectacled lawyer. She also appeared with Jet Lee in *The Master*.

filmography

1987	Dragons Forever
1989	Four Loves
	All Night Long
1990	Doctor Vampire
	Will of Iron
1992	The Master

lee heung kin

Lee Heung Kin was born in 1930 and practiced Chinese Opera from the age of 16. In 1956 she stepped into the film industry, where she was cast in the film *Wong Fei Hung 3*. She also appeared in *Armed Escort* (1956). Up until now she has starred and co-starred in hundreds of films and her talent lies in portraying wicked characters, especially ill-hearted concubines. She joined TVB in 1972 where she starred in and hosted a number of TV dramas and shows.

filmography

1956	Wong Fei Hung 3
	Armed Escort
1983	Hong Kong Singer
1985	Musical Singer
1986	Sweet Surrender
	The Family Strikes Back
	A Hearty Response
1987	The Big Brother
1988	Couples Couples Couples
	Mistaken Identity
	On the Run
	Love Soldier of Fortune
	Keep on Dancing
1992	All's Well that Ends Well
1994	It's a Wonderful Life

李若彤 lee yuk tong

Lee Yuk Tong once worked as an air stewardess and model. She was noticed by maverick director Tsui Hark when he was casting for the Manga-in-Motion flick *The Wicked City*, which he produced, where she was cast alongside Michelle Reis. Her performance proved solid enough to trigger off a career as an actress.

filmography

1992	The Wicked City
1994	Burning Paradise
	The Final Option
	Victory
	Awakening

Burning Paradise

marianna hung

Hong **K**ong **a**ctress who has appeared in several Category III thrillers. Films include *Red Shield* (1992), *Friday Gigolo* (1992), *Malevolent Male* (1993), *Days of Tomorrow* (1993) and *Obsession* (1993).

keung yung

Keung Yung appeared in five or six TV dramas and advertisements in Shanghai before she came to Hong Kong in 1984. Later she joined Golden Harvest and appeared in the all-star cast line-up for *Future Cops*.

姜蓉 **filmography**

1993	Future Cops
1994	The Third Full Moon
	How Deep is Your Love
	The Crucifixion

黎姿 gigi lai

A little known actress in the West who has starred in several critically acclaimed films. Her big break came when she starred alongside Andy Lau in *Dragon in Jail* (1990). She also starred in the Amy Yip drama *Queen of the Underworld* and in Wong Jing's new wave martial arts flick *Kung Fu Cult Master*.

filmography

1990	Dragon in Jail
1991	Spiritual Trinity
	Queen of the Underworld
1993	Kung Fu Cult Master
1995	Full Throttle
1996	Sixty Million Dollar Man

isabelle chow

Isabelle Chow may have been overshadowed by buxom actress Amy Yip in Golden Harvest's *Sex and Zen*, but she is still well worth a picture in any book dealing with Asian babes. Even though at this stage we are running low on space in the book she just had to go in. Do you blame us!

周弘

Isabelle Chow goes under the whip in Sex and Zen

---

julie lee

李華月

Julie Lee, or Lee May Fung, is yet another ravishing sleazy Category III starlet who has yet to be given top billing. Cast in films like *A Chinese Torture Chamber* (1994), *Love to Kill* (1994) and *Portrait of a Serial Rapist* (1994), she is a woman who can take her abuse and often plays the victim of a brutal rape. Julie has appeared in many Chinese magazines baring all, often bound by ropes. She likes to shock, off screen as well as on, and openly admits to having a fascination with the darker side of sex, but despite her willingness to do whatever the script calls for, producers and directors seem to think that at forty years of age she may be a tad over the hill. But if she came knocking at your bedroom door would you tell her to go away?

filmography

1992	Emotional Girl
1994	Love to Kill
	Portrait of a Serial Rapist
	1941: Hong Kong on Fire
	A Chinese Torture Chamber

---

winnie lau

Winnie Lau is more famous for her singing, and for those of you who have a karaoke machine, it's possible that you've belted out a few of her tunes. Her most memorable movie role is in *Widow Warriors*, which is available on video in the UK. But if you want a better look at Winnie, her photo used to frequently appear in the many Hong Kong music magazines, and she can be found on the *YES Music Star* trading cards. Either way, it's a visit to your local Chinatown.

劉小慧

pak ka shin

Pak Ka Shin was the champion in the Carlsberg Singing Contest in 1995 and has so far released four albums, the last of which was marketed as a personal album. She made her first and only screen appearance in the attention-getting film *Twenty Something* in 1994.

葉蒨文 sally yeh / yip

Sally Yeh (Yip Tse Man) grew up in Canada and in 1980 relocated to her native country, Taiwan, where she embarked upon a highly successful singing career. Her music made a huge impact and she released two best selling albums. King of schlock, director Chu Yen Ping, was quick to cash in on Sally's gorgeous face and curvaceous figure, not to mention her ever-growing popularity, and cast her in a number of big budget Taiwan flicks such as *Golden Queen Commando* and *Seven Foxes*, alongside Brigitte Lin (both 1981). Sally then moved to Hong Kong, where she started to record her songs in Cantonese. She soon enjoyed the same level of success she had achieved in Taiwan.

She also continued her film career and began to star in big Hong Kong movie productions like *Mr Boo 6: Teppanyaki* (1982), Ringo Lam's *Cupid One* (1985) and Tsui Hark's *Peking Opera Blues*

Sally Yeh goes bionic in Roboforce

(1986) and *I Love Maria* aka *Roboforce* (1988). But without doubt Sally's best known performance is that of the partially blinded singer in John Woo's classic *The Killer* (1989). Currently Sally resides in Hong Kong where she still records, and it is reported that she plans to marry Hong Kong actor and singer George Lam.

Below: Sally Yeh gets caught up in a mexican stand-off/tea party between Chow Yun Fat and Danny Lee in The Killer

Sally Yeh shoots to kill in Roboforce

sally yip / yeh

葉蒨文

filmography

1982	Mariana
	Mr Boo 6: Teppanyaki
1984	Golden Queen Commando
	Seven Foxes
	The Occupant
1985	Cupid One
1986	The Protector (Hong Kong version)
	Peking Opera Blues
1987	Shanghai Blues
1988	Roboforce aka I Love Maria
	Diary of a Big Man
1989	The Killer
198?	Just For Fun
1991	Sisters of the World Unite

Sally Yeh with Chow Yun Fat in The Killer

呂少玲 elaine liu

Elaine Liu (Liu Siu Ling) made her dramatic first appearance on the Jade Screen in the classic femme fatale film *Angel* (1988), with kung fu movie queens Yukari Oshima and Moon Lee. The international impact of this movie has obviously brought Elaine to the attention of the western public as the femme fatale genre has begun to attract more and more interest. Her instant success led to her returning to star alongside Yukari Oshima in the sequel, *Angel 2*, in 1989. She also starred in the lesser known but superb action flick *The Innocent Interloper* (1990), directed by Wang Lung Wei. She put in a notable performance in *Bullet For Hire* (1991) alongside Simon Yam and Jackie Cheung, playing a beautiful Chinese bodyguard. More recently she has starred in *Once Upon A Time in China 5* (1994), and as the cold-blooded terrorist in Yuen Woo Ping's *Red Wolf* (1995), a highly recommended all-out action flick in the vein of *In The Line of Duty 4* and *Tiger Cage*.

filmography

1988	Angel
1989	Angel 2
1990	Innocent Interloper
1991	Bullet For Hire
	Stone Age Warriors
1992	Rich Man
1994	Once Upon A Time in China 5
1995	Red Wolf

Elaine Liu gets trigger happy in Red Wolf

the essential guide to deadly china dolls • **187**

子悦美穗志 etsuko shiomi

Etsuko Shiomi, better known as Sue Shiomi, is a Japanese femme fatale who was finding fame on the big screen long before the likes of Yukari Oshima and Michiko Nishiwaki. For those who follow the Japanese scene avidly, she is best known for her roles in *Golgo 13 – Kowloon Assignment* and *Kikaider 01*, which I'm afraid I have very little knowledge of. From a martial arts point of view, in the UK Sue is best known as the co-star in the Sonny Chiba *Streetfighter* movies and took the lead in *Sister Streetfighter*. She has also made plenty of Japanese chambara movies. Her filmography is too vast even to undertake to research, but as I am fond of the Sonny Chiba movies and she is an action femme fatale, she justly deserves her place in this book.

filmography

1975	Karate Bullfighter
1976	The Streetfighter
	Sister Streetfighter
1977	Streetfighter's Last Revenge
	Golgo 13 – Kowloon Assignment
	The Killing Machine
1978	A Dynamite Kick
	Return of Sister Streetfighter
1980	Dragon Princess
1982	Shogun's Ninja
	Roaring Fire
1984	Legend of the Eight Samurai
?	Kikaider 01

甘家鳳 phoenix chen

The only recognised kung fu sister of Jackie Chan and Samo Hung, Phoenix Chen, or Kan Chia Fong, started training in Peking Opera when she was seven and like the other kids quickly made the transition from the stage to the big screen, where she gave Jackie a good beating in *Police Woman*, aka *Young Tiger*. She married director Lo Chun Ku and appeared in several of his films, including *Dragon Claws* and *Bastard Swordsman*.

Phoenix Chen in Dreadnaught

filmography

1973	Police Woman
1975	Black Dragon Revenge – the Death of Bruce Lee
1978	Dragon Claws
	Dragon Lee and the Five Brothers
1979	Fearless Duo
	The Dragon and the Young Master
1982	The Dragon, the Young Master
	Bastard Swordsman
1983	Dreadnaught

林小樓 lin shao lou aka Sharon Foster

Standing only 5'1" tall, Lin Shao Lou, or the Peach Baby as she is sometimes known, studied Peking Opera at the Lu Kwong Opera Academy in downtown Taipei. Her first film, *Child of Peach*, was a huge success and three sequels followed. She didn't find the same amount of success in the modern day genre. Lin is currently working on Taiwanese cable and television in swordplay serials.

filmography

1985	Child of Peach
1986	Return of the Child of Peach
1987	Fiery Phoenix
	Heroic Fight
1988	Kung Fu Wonderchild
	King of Kids
1989	Thunder Cops
	Twelve Fairies
	Punk Police
1990	The Master and I
1991	The Magic Amethyst
	Dignified Killers
1995	Horrible High Heels

Kung Fu Wonderchild

Child of Peach

徐楓

hsu feng

The first film Hsu Feng had a starring role in was the international hit *A Touch of Zen*, where her performance so captivated audiences far and wide that Kung Hu quickly cast her in *The Valiant Ones*. Hsu made dozens of Taiwan-made swordplay pictures in the seventies but none had the impact of her films for King Hu. In the mid eighties Hsu Feng turned to producing and had great success with the *Kung Fu Kids* series. Most recently she enjoyed success with *Farewell My Concubine*, which won the Palm d'Or award at Cannes in 1994.

Hsu Feng with Jackie Chan in To Kill With Intrigue

The Assassin

filmography

1971	The Invincible Sword
1972	The Fate of Lee Khan
1974	Sex, Love and Hate
	With Them All
	Chase Step By Step
1975	Dragon Gate
	Seven Spirit Pagoda
	The Assassin
	Women Soldiers
1976	Shaolin Kung Fu Mystigogue
	A Touch of Zen
	The Valiant Ones
	The Greatest Plot
1977	Killer, Killer, Killer
	The Chivalry, the Gunmen
	and the Killer
	To Kill With Intrigue
1979	The Revenger
	Raining on the Mountain
1985–90	Kung Fu Kids 1-4 (prod)
1994	Farewell My Concubine (prod)
1996	Tempestuous Moon (prod)

wong hang sau

Cute as a button and as crisp as a biscuit, Cecilia Wong Hang Sau started working for the ex-manager of Cathay Studios, Yeow Ban Yee, in his film *Way of the Black Dragon*, where she played opposite the great 'Black Dragon' himself Ron Van Clief. Following this picture she starred in what still remains the best Wing Chun bio-pic yet, *Stranger From Shaolin*. Her performance in the film brought her to the attention of Shaw Brothers kung fu master Liu Chia Liang and he cast her as the spoilt daughter of the patriotic Tien Clan in *Shaolin Mantis*, followed by *Spiritual Boxer 2*.
Cecilia worked freelance for most of the seventies, appearing with Samo Hung and Tung Wei in *The Invincible Kung Fu Master* and the First Films cult classic *Four Invincibles*. During the eighties Ms Wong found a home at TVB where she was one of the most popular artistes. She has now retired from acting to spend her time looking after her showbiz husband Nat 'Lolanto' Chan.

黃杏秀

The deadly Wong Hang Sau in The Magnificent Kick

Incredible Kung Fu Master

Wong Hang Sau strikes a pose in Shaolin Ex-Monk

Shaolin Mantis

filmography

1975	Way of the Black Dragon
1976	The Hunter
	The Butterfly and the Crocodile
1977	Shaolin Mantis
	Spiritual Boxer 2
1978	Shaolin Ex-Monk
	Dirty Kung Fu
1979	Incredible Kung Fu Master
	Four Invincibles
	The Magnificent Kick
	Young Avenger
1980	My Rebellious Son
1981	Young Heroes (TV)
	Woman Stuntman
?	Stranger From Shaolin

龍君兒
dorris lung jun er

Dorris Lung Jun Er's film career began in 1976 in Taiwanese productions such as *Shaolin Wooden Men*, *Chivalrous Inn* and *One Armed Boxer Versus the Flying Guillotine*. She appeared in over sixty Taiwanese productions including *Half a Loaf of Kung Fu* with Jackie Chan. Due to her unstable character and three suicide attempts producers were reluctant to cast her in any further productions.

Hero of the Wild

Dorris kicks out in Half a Loaf of Kung Fu

filmography

1976	Shaolin Wooden Men
	One Armed Boxer Versus the Flying Guillotine
	Eunuch of Western Palace
1977	Knife of Devil's Soul
	Clutch of Power
	Golden Mask
	Rebel of Shaolin
	Eight Masters
	Chivalrous Inn
	Duel with the Devil
	The Flash Legs
	Two Assassins of the Darkness
	Along Came the Tiger
	Best of Shaolin Kung Fu
1978	Half a Loaf of Kung Fu
	The Magnificent
	Born to Fight
	Travelling Swordsman of Thunder
	18 Bronze Girls of Shaolin
	Jade Fox
	Hero of the Wild
	Secret Message
1979	Heroes' Tears
	Shaolin Heroes
	Jade Dagger
	aka Jade Dagger Ninja

Lung Jun Er claws out at a baby Wong Yat Lung in Jade Fox

Left: Hwa Ling strikes out in The Avenging Boxing

華玲

hwa ling

Peking Opera trained, Hwa Ling made her movie debut in Karl Mak's *The Good, the Bad and the Loser*. This was followed by tremendous performances in *Kung Fu of Tamo Style* and *Fatal Needles, Fatal Fists*.

filmography

1977	The Good, the Bad and the Loser
	Eagle's Claw
1978	Fatal Needles, Fatal Fists
	Kung Fu of Tamo Style
1979	The Avenging Boxing

filmography

1965	The Duck Breeders
1966	My Land is My Country
1968	Tomorrow is Another Day
	Hellgate
	Dear Murderer
	The Millionaire Chase
1970	Never Too Late to Mend
1971	Stranger in Hong Kong
	The Yellow Muffler
	The Night is
	Young
1975	Bruce Lee
	and I
	Stoner
	The Evidence
	The Virgin
	Mart
	Queen's
	Ransom
1978	Mysterious
	Footworks of Kung Fu

丁珮

betty ting pei

Born in Taiwan, Betty Ting Pei (Tang Mei Li) quickly blossomed into a true sex kitten and was soon snapped up by the Shaw Brothers Studio, where she appeared in countless scandalous sexploitation movies. But Betty's claim to international fame came when rumours began to circulate that she was having an affair with Bruce Lee. It was her bad luck that Bruce Lee, the fittest man alive, died in her apartment in 1973. Years later, Betty wrote and starred in the Shaw Brothers tribute, aptly titled *Bruce Lee and I*, with Danny Lee (*The Killer*). Betty married Hong Kong big boss Charles Heung, sadly divorcing some time later. Betty is now a devout buddhist and has not made a film in years.

胡錦 hu chin

Win them All

The quintessential sexy temptress who portrayed brothel madams or casino bosses, Hu Chin was born on June 2, 1947 and studied Peking Opera in Taipei. She found stardom in 1969 when she played a number of sexy roles in Shaw Brothers films, most notably *The Golden Lotus* alongside Jackie Chan.

filmography

1972	The Fate of Lee Khan
	Bandits From Shangtung
	The Great Warlord
1973	The Golden Lotus
	Illicit Desire
	Drug Gang
	Northern Ladies of China
	House of 72 Tenants
	Tornado of Pearl River
1974	Sinful Confessions
	Kidnap
	Win Them All
	Wine, Women and Song
	Supreme
1975	Boxer Rebellion
	Fantastic Magic Baby
	The Gambling Syndicate
	The Virgin Mart
1976	Love and Nature
	Low Society
	Moods of Love
	Tiger Love
	Wrong Side of the Track
	Valley of the Butterfly
1977	Layout
	Dream of the Red Chamber
	Golden Nun
1978	Dreaming Fists, Slender Hands

Hu Chin with Jenny in The Golden Lotus

wang ping

filmography

汪萍

This cute Taiwanese actress started out with the Shaw Brothers Studio, appearing in such classics as *The Chinese Boxer*, with Jimmy Wang Yu, and *The Killer*. Like Wang Yu she left the Shaw Brothers in the early seventies and furthered her career in Taiwan.

1969	The Chinese Boxer
1970	The Duel
	Vengeance
1972	The Killer
	Duel for Gold
	The One Armed Boxer
	Beauty Heroine

chang ling

張玲

This mad woman from Taiwan started her film career in the early seventies, starring in kung fu classics like *Fist From Shaolin* (1974), alongside Pai Ying. She found superstardom in Taiwan when she appeared on television in a collection of swordplay dramas which quickly span off into film versions. She is perhaps best known to the western audience for her bizarre cult films like *Wolf Devil Woman* (1980) and *Dark Lady of Kung Fu* (1980).

My Blade My Life

My Blade My Life

Matching Escort

filmography

1974	Fist From Shaolin
1976	Men on the Hour
1977	My Blade My Life
	Witty Hand Witty Sword
	King of Money and Fists
1980	Wolf Devil Woman
	Dark Lady of Kung Fu
	Miraculous Flower
	General Invincible
1981	Blazing Paradise
1982	Hero at Border Region
	Inheritor of Kung Fu
?	Matching Escort

yang ching ching

楊菁菁

Born on Hainan Island, China, Yang Ching Ching was spotted by Liu Chia Liang at a Wu Shu demonstration and signed up. She appeared most notably in *Fist of the White Lotus* and *Return to the 36th Chamber of Shaolin*. Ching Ching is the only female choreographer working in Hong Kong. She mostly spends her time at ATV nowadays.

filmography

1979	Fist of the White Lotus
	Two Champions of Shaolin
1980	Return to the 36th Chamber
1982	Eight Diagram Pole Fighter
1983	Bastard Swordsman
	Lady Assassin
1984	Thunderclap
1989	Licence to Steal
1993	Setting Sun

文雪兒 candy wen

Candy Wen Man Suet Yee was first noticed by director Chu Yuan when she was visiting her friends who were filming at the Shaw Brothers Studio. This chance visit quickly led to her being given a contract to sign, whereupon she immediately found a steady stream of work. She also found further popularity and fame on Hong Kong TV.

filmography

1978	Heaven Sword and Dragon Sabre
	The Swordsman and the Enchantress
1979	Lover's Blade
	Two Champions of Shaolin
	The Master
	Crazy Horse Intelligent Monkey
	Tiger Over Wall
	Kid With a Tattoo
	Proud Twins
1980	Sword Stained With Royal Blood
	Emperor and his Brother
1982	The Cheeky Chap
198?	Holy Flame in the Martial World

Lover's Blade

張天愛 flora cheng

Educated in England, Flora Cheng Tien Ai was originally a ballet dancer before turning to movies. Her first films were for Golden Harvest and include *Duel to the Death* and director Patrick Tam's *The Sword*. Flora seldom appears in films nowadays since she leads a very active business life.

filmography

1980	The Sword
	Return of the Deadly Blade
1981	Duel to the Death
	Super Fool
?	Life After Life
?	Expensive Tastes

Flora Cheng in Duel to the Death, with Tsui Siu Keung

nora miao

Nora Miao is of Eurasian descent and was first introduced to Western audiences when she appeared in Bruce Lee's first major motion picture *The Big Boss*. Her reputation was further enhanced when Bruce invited her back to co-star as his on-screen love interest in *Fist of Fury*. Their first passionate on-screen kiss was to be one of the first to appear in a martial arts film. Nora also co-starred in Bruce's directorial debut film *Way of the Dragon*.

Nora has appeared and co-starred in her fair share of kung fu/swordplay pictures, which included three co-starring roles alongside Jackie Chan, the best being *Snake and Crane Arts of Shaolin*. Nora retired in the early eighties and resides on Hong Kong island. She was recently lured out of retirement to appear in the Lo Wei tribute film *How to Meet the Lucky Stars*.

Nora Miao with Bruce lee in Way of the Dragon?

The Blade Spares None

New Fist of Fury

filmography

1971	The Big Boss
1972	The Comet Strikes
	Invincible Eight
	Fist of Fury
	The Hurricane
	The Blade Spares None
	Way of the Dragon
1973	Skyhawk
1974	Naughty Naughty
1975	Bruce's Fingers
	Showdown at the Equator
	Showdown at the Equator
	Kung Fu Kid
1976	New Fist of Fury
	Handcuff
1977	Snake and Crane Arts of Shaolin
	Dragon Fist
1978	Samurai Death Belt
	To Kill a Jaguar
	My Blade My Life
1979	The Last Duel
197?	The Devil's Treasure
1996	How to Meet the Lucky Stars

米雪 michelle lai

Michelle Lai Mai Suet is a striking dark-skinned beauty whose popularity arose from the thousands of hours of Hong Kong television that she appeared in. Even today she is still popular on television. Michelle also found time to carve out a career in the movie industry, appearing mostly in kung fu movies during the seventies.

filmography

1977	Ten Tigers of Shaolin
1978	Kung Fu Versus Yoga
	Edge of Fury
	The Star, the Rogue and the Kung Fu Kid
1979	Twins of Kung Fu
	Funny Kung Fu
	36 Crazy Fists
1980	108 Killer aka Blow Up
	The Butterfly Murders
1981	Gang Master

孟秋 kitty meng

Kitty Meng Chiao is the older sister of kung fu star/action choreographer Meng Hoi. Her career saw her feature in many martial arts movies, especially in the early to mid seventies. She has also appeared in modern day films, including *Angel Enforcers*.

Iron Bull

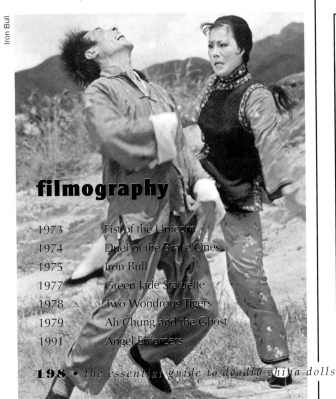

filmography

1973	Fist of the Unicorn
1974	Duel of the Brave Ones
1975	Iron Bull
1977	Green Jade Statuette
1978	Two Wondrous Tigers
1979	Ah Chung and the Ghost
1991	Angel Enforcers

yuan chu 元菊

This gifted acrobatic performer is the younger classmate of Jackie Chan and Phoenix Chen from their Peking Opera School days. Her opening fight sequence in *Fearless Duo* (1978) where she demonstrated the fairy fist technique brought audiences at the time to their feet. Sadly this talented actress made only two films, the other being *Young Hero* (1978).

Young Hero

lin fong chiao

Lin Fong Chiao has to be regarded as the absolute movie queen from Taiwan. During her career Lin appeared in hundreds of love story dramas which were popular throughout the seventies. Her movies generated millions of dollars and her popularity and status elevated her to that of Taiwanese darling. In 1981 she retired from movies and it was at this point she embarked on a romance with Jackie Chan which resulted in their marriage one year later. They had one son but sadly the marriage broke down and they are now divorced.

林鳳嬌

Eternal Love

filmography

1973	Chinese Kung Fu
1974	Hero of the Waterfront
1975	Our Land, Our People
	Land of the Undaunted
1976	The Waves
	Coincidence
	Love Popcorn
	A Lovely Morning Engagement
1977	We Feel the Wind Again
	Eternal Love
1978	Another Day Another Evening
	A Boat in the Ocean
	The War of the Sexes

pauline yeung

Pauline Yeung Bo Ling was born on the 17th April 1967. Her career as a model led to her winning the Miss Hong Kong Beauty Pageant and her success led to a recording contract. She also pursued an acting career, making her debut appearance alongside Jackie Chan, Samo Hung and Phillip Ko in *Dragons Forever* (1987), using a microphone as improvised nunchakus. She also co-starred with Donnie Yen in the erotic Category III flick *Holy Virgin Versus the Evil Dead* (1990) and also appeared in the under-rated *Happy Ghost 4* (1991).

湯寶如

Holy Virgin Versus the Evil Dead

er, nunchakus???

Dragons Forever

filmography

Holy Virgin Versus the Evil Dead

1987	Dragons Forever
1989	Dream of Desire
	How To Be a Millionaire
	Four Loves
1990	Holy Virgin Versus the Evil Dead
1991	Return of the Evil Fox
	Happy Ghost 4

The Holy Virgin versus The Evil Dead

栢安妮 ann bridgewater

Ann Bridgewater (Bak An Ni) was formerly a champion ice skater and is of European descent. She will be best remembered for her role in *Top Squad*, aka *The Inspector Wears a Skirt*, and as the girlfriend of Chow Yun Fat in Ringo Lam's *Full Contact*, where this stunning beauty can be seen driving audiences wild with her Hong Kong showgirl style dancing. Ann also co-starred with Chow Sing Chi and Jacky Cheung in the under-rated *Curry and Pepper*.

A distressed Ann Bridgewater in Full Contact

filmography

1988	The Inspector Wears a Skirt aka Top Squad
1989	Thunder Squad aka Operation Pink Squad
	Thunder Squad 2 aka Operation Pink Squad 2
	The Inspector Wears a Skirt 2
198?	I Do
198?	Fatal Love
198?	The Isle of Fantasy
1990	My Hero
1991	Curry and Pepper
1992	Full Contact
1994	Abracadabra
199?	Tricky Gambler
199?	Trouble Couples

Thunder Squad

符鈺晶 bonnie fu

A worthy mention in this 'tit bit' section for Bonnie whose curvaceous figure oozes sex appeal. She will certainly be remembered by anybody who has seen Ringo Lam's *Full Contact* (1992), where she played the micro-mini-skirted slut 'Virgin'. She also co-starred alongside Jacky Cheung and Lam Ching Ying in *Hot Hot and Pom Pom*, aka *Hong Kong Lethal Weapon* (1992).

filmography

1992	Full Contact
	Hot Hot and Pom Pom

Hot Hot and Pom Pom

Bonnie Fu (left) is joined by Ann Bridgewater and Anthony Wong in Full Contact

Full Contact

may law

Born on the 9th January 1966 and the star of the first instalment of the *Happy Ghost* series, this beautiful actress recently won the heart of Canto-pop singer/actor Jacky Cheung, whom she married in London during his concert tour of the UK in 1995. Anybody wanting to know what the new Mrs Cheung looks like should check out *Return Engagement*, *Midnight Angel* or *The Last Blood*, all released in the UK.

羅美薇

filmography

198?	Happy Ghost
198?	Happy Ghost 2
1990	Return Engagement
1991	Midnight Angel
1992	The Last Blood
	Operation Scorpio
	aka Scorpion King
	Once a Black Sheep
	Lady Supercop
?	Story of Kennedy Town

May Law shoots to kill and chain smoke in *Once a Black Sheep*

葉芳華

francoise yip

Wild

Rumble in the Bronx

Newcomer Francoise Yip Fong Wah had Western temperatures rising when she co-starred with Jackie Chan in *Rumble in the Bronx* (1995). She will be a name to watch out for and has recently co-starred in the adult drama flick *Wild* (1996). A babe to definitely keep an eye out for.

emily chu

朱寶意

Emily Chu was born on 31st October 1960. Raised and educated in Northern California she later moved back to Hong Kong where she pursued a career as a model and later found herself acting on Hong Kong television. She was signed by Golden Harvest and co-starred alongside Jackie Chan in *Heart of the Dragon* aka *First Mission*. She also played Leslie Cheung's wife in *A Better Tomorrow* parts 1 and 2.

Jackie Chan and Emily Chu get cosy in First Mission

filmography

198?	Vampire's Breakfast
198?	Big Brother
1985	Scared Stiff
	Heart of the Dragon
	aka First Mission
1986	A Better Tomorrow
1987	A Better Tomorrow 2
	Witch From Nepal
	Return of the Demon
1988	Rouge
1990	Ghostly Love
	Angel or Whore
1991	Dignified Killers
199?	Death Comes in Dreams

honourable mentions

WITH TITLES OF FILMS FOR WHICH THEY ARE BEST KNOWN

kam fong ling 金鳳玲
Ape Girl

pan yin tze 潘紫迎
One Armed Swordsman

sydney 雪梨
Dragon Lord

chu yin 朱茵
A Chinese Odyssey

lin chen chi 林珍奇
Battle Wizard

regina kent 簡慧珍
Legacy of Rage

liu rei chi 劉瑞琪
Lunatic Frog Woman

pat ha 夏文汐
On the Run

meg lam 林建明
Master Strikes

judy ong 翁倩玉
Zu: Warriors From the Magic Mountain

lu hsiu ling 呂娇菱
Rosa

yi suk kwan 倪淑君
Esprit D'Amour

olivia cheng 鄭文雅
Why Me?

goto kumiko 後藤久美子
City Hunter

wong chiu yin 黃秋燕
Shaolin Temple 2: Kids From Shaolin

rena murakami
Escape From Brothel

shaw may chi 召美琪
Sting of the Scorpion

leung tse man 梁思敏
Basic Impulse

fennie yuen 袁潔瑩
Nightlife Hero

Cynthia Rothrock's contribution to Martial Arts Movies by Tony Rayner

No reference book about battling babes would be complete without a comprehensive acknowledgement to the only non-Chinese actress to really make an impact on the Martial Arts scene and she is the 5'3" champion from Wilmington, Delaware – Cynthia Rothrock! I do not intend to merely reiterate yards of facts of which fans will be already well aware, instead this dedication will attempt to unravel the maze of differences in her video releases, thereby posing an intriguing challenge to 'completists'.

A quick recap on history first! In 1983 Golden Harvest casting directors came to LA (from Hong Kong, in case anybody doesn't know) to search for the next Bruce Lee. Although the call was for men, Cynthia attended and the folks from G.H. quickly changed their minds and whisked her off to HK to star in *Yes Madam*. Her outstanding achievements in competition had earned her five black belts in Women's North American Forms and Weapons and at the time of the auditions, she was working with the West Coast Demonstration team.

filmography

1985 *Yes Madam*
UK title is *Police Assassins 2* , not to be confused with *Yes Madam '92*, with Cynthia Khan! The first *Police Assassins* movie had starred Michelle Khan and was the UK title for *In the Line of Duty 2*, also known as *Royal Warriors*! There has been enough confusion about the 'Khans' and the *In the Line of Duty* series so I won't digress!!! The original Hong Kong version of *Yes, Madam* has more dialogue than the UK one and the Cantonese speech is a little easier on the ear than the dubbed version! *24 Hours to Midnight* is also listed in another filmography but it should probably be filed away as 'pitfalls of starting out in the business'.

1986 *Shanghai Express* aka *Millionaires Express*
Not much confusion there!
No Retreat, No Surrender 2 is mistakenly listed as just *No Retreat, No Surrender* in the Fan Club filmography and it is known as *Raging Thunder* in the US!
Righting Wrongs came out as *Above the Law* in UK but in Argentina it's called *Veredicto de Sangre*. Sleeve shows Cynthia aiming a high kick at Jeff Wincott (who isn't even in it) with the Statue of Liberty in the background! The director is supposedly 'Anthony John Denison' – I wonder if Cory Yuen knows that???!

1987 *Magic Crystal* is inexplicably confused with *Fight to Win* in a 1993 interview, but it was a completely different film released by Imperial Entertainment in the UK in 1991.

1988 A busy year
China O'Brien 1 & 2
Top Squad aka *The Inspector Wears a Skirt*
Blonde Fury (aka *Lady Reporter*, aka *Above the Law 2*) and an obscurity called *Key Witness*.

1989 *Triple Cross* (*Angel of Fury* in the US). The American version has a pre-credit torture by drill sequence which is missing from the Australian one but there is a long chase sequence involving rushing over a roof top and descending by rope edited in the US version!
Martial Law was Cynthia's first movie shot in LA. Back overseas for *Prince of the Sun*, scheduled for a 1996 UK release.
Attended an event organised by *Eastern Heroes* in the UK where a triple bill of her movies was screened – *The Inspector Wears a Skirt*, *Blonde Fury* and *Shanghai Express*. Attended a meal in her honour and gave martial arts lessons to a crowd of hungry fans.

1990 *City Cops* (Hong Kong) – issued in UK as *Beyond the Law*, subsequently re-issued under its original title, and re-issued in Hong Kong as *Free Fighter*, thus resulting in the unwary ending up with three copies of the same film!

1990 A frantic output saw: *Fast Getaway* (it prompted a sequel) – *Martial Law 2*, *Lady Dragon*, *Tiger Claws* and *Rage and Honour*

1991 A visit to UK for a Martial Arts Extravaganza in Birmingham, captured on tape by First Independent. *Rage & Honour 2*, *Lady Dragon 2* (*Angel of Fury* in the UK) and *Honour & Glory* followed. However, in 1992 the illustrious Godfrey Ho acquired *Honour & Glory* and cobbled together some unreleased footage from a Waise Lee actioner, plus various fight-scenes with Yukari Oshima, releasing the final blend as *Angel the Kickboxer*. Nice widescreen print, even if the two storylines are a bit confusing!

1992 A dramatic departure from conventional fight movies with a Martial Arts/Horror movie called *Undefeatable*.

1993 *Irresistible Force* was a TV pilot made in Australia, which regrettably didn't turn into a series. It runs about 73 minutes on video. Two feature movies followed: *Guardian Angel* and *Eye for an Eye*.

1994 *Dark Red* was discussed, casting Cynthia as a psychopathic killer, featuring no martial arts. Artwork for a poster was designed but as yet the project hasn't materialised.

1996 filming began on *Blonde Justice* in LA in February and a cunningly retitled US TV documentary called *Encyclopedia* (their spelling!) *of Martial Arts – Vol. 1* was released as *Martial Combat*!

Future projects: *Tiger Claws 2* and *Lady Steele*.

TV shows in the UK that have featured Cynthia: twice on *The Little Picture Show* and a brief spot on the short-lived *Girlie Show*.

Lady Dragon

Indispensable sources for reading up : *The Essential guide to Hong Kong Movies*, *She* issue 4, *Impact* magazine (3 issues with interviews), *Australian Video Trader* and a revealing(!) spread in *Femme Fatales*.

With such an impressive catalogue it is now plain to see that no other non-Chinese actress has achieved as much as Cynthia and it remains to be seen if she can crack the mainstream success she so richly deserves.

Shanghai Express

Cynthia with Richard Norton and Keith
Cook on the set of China O'Brien

category III

What's your pleasure? Rena Murakami is open to suggestions in Escape from Brothel

sex & zen

text:
Howard Lake

"I feel like millions of ants biting my private parts..."

— *(Sex & Zen)*

As with much of what passes for history when it comes to Hong Kong cinema, a fog of confusion shrouds the genesis of HK's answer to the Western X/18 movie, Category III, but it is generally accepted that the genre first emerged at the tail-end of the1980s as local filmmakers took note of the box office success enjoyed by steamy Hollywood potboilers such as *Basic Instinct* and *Fatal Attraction*, films which had considerably upped the ante in respect of how much sex 'n' violence a sex 'n' violence movie should contain.

Never slow to appropriate a trend, Hong Kong producers hurriedly clambered aboard the bandwagon, intent upon apeing the style (and, ergo, the financial success) of these American trailblazers.

Women on top... Devil Girl 18

Lau Ka's *The Black Wall* (1989) was reputedly one of the first out of the blocks, starring Lawrence Ng and Lau Ka Bung, although earlier works, for example *Night Caller* (1987), directed by Phillip Chan and starring Pauline Wong, would have been categorised as a Cat III movie.

These movies were fairly slavish in their aping of Hollywood style, but that was not to say that Hong Kong cinema didn't have traditions of its own to tap into. Ghost and supernatural horror movies had long had a keen following among local audiences and, as was a feature of much of Hammer's output in their sixties heyday, no spooky picture was complete without its sexy, shrieking starlet. Yet as Hammer discovered when social mores changed and permissiveness took hold, that a dollop of spicier action made a palatable

condiment to the more grisly main course, likewise one of the first Hong Kong genres to take on board a more relaxed attitude to matters carnal was fantasy-horror, with *Holy Virgin Versus the Evil Dead* (1990) being one of the earliest examples. Directed by Choy Fat, starring Donnie Yen and Sibelle Hu, this gained a Cat III rating more by virtue of its gut-ripping gore than any excessive sexual shenanigans. For that, you have to turn to Chan Li's *The Curse* (1990), an often-overlooked picture, but still interesting for its contribution to genre-history (rather than the rarely-clothed performance of star Li Sua naturally) in the way a supernatural storyline is utilized as an excuse for acres of underclad female flesh.

While this new breed of films had considerably more grit and guts (often literally) than the more conservative fare which had preceded it, producers saw little purpose in gaining a Cat III certification solely on the grounds of violence. The rationale was: if your film was to be awarded restricted status anyway, why not go the whole hog and get really down 'n' dirty? Thus was born a genre of film which constituted a genuine first for the Hong Kong industry: the fully-fledged, honest-to-god sex movie.

"Thugs don't normally frontally attack our chests..."

— *(Robotrix)*

As the Nineties began, more and more producers and stars shed their inhibitions and foundation garments as the trickle of Cat III product became a flood, with titles such as *Ghostly Vixen* (1989), the movie which first alerted fans to a certain Ms. Yip, Ho Fan's *Erotic Nights* (1989) and *Temptation Summary* (1990), David Lam's *Hong Kong Gigolo* (1990) and Wu Kwo Rem's *Ghostly Love* (1990), the latter supernatural potboiler being probably the best, which had audiences (especially the male element) becoming increasingly hot under the collar. However, these films were mostly the work of maverick producers operating independently of the major companies, the bulk of which were carefully keeping tabs on the burgeoning Cat III output, keen to check which way the wind was blowing and, more importantly, whether there was any money in all this kit-off, sweaty-limbed shenanigans.

Clearly, on both counts they were satisfied for before 1990 was out Diagonal Pictures, from the Golden Harvest camp, had entered the fray with *Erotic Ghost Story*, directed by Nan Nai Choi and starring the genre's first outstanding (the double-entendre is intended) star, the awesomely comely former TV actress, Amy Yip. The steamy saga which launched a trilogy was thin on plot and often clumsily staged, but in fulfilling its raison d'etre of delivering large segments of undraped sensual action, lovingly and explicitly (even considering the criteria outlined above) filmed, *Erotic Ghost Story* hit the mark with a resounding thud, coining an impressive HK$12m on its theatrical release. The word was out: softcore sex sold and, furthermore, softcore sex starring Amy Yip sold even better.

Yip it was who led the assault of the Cat III babes on the theatrical marketplace and '91 proved to be, without doubt, her year.

Supergang, starring Bruce Li

Robotrix, with its HK$6m take was just the foretaste of what was to come. *Sex and Zen* really took the lid (and plenty else besides) off the raunchy new rating. The importance of Michael Mak's movie cannot be underestimated, both for its impact on the career of Amy Yip and for its influence on the direction Category III movies would take (for greater detail on this blockbuster, see the section on Amy Yip).

Witchcraft vs. Curse (1991) was another title to perform well alongside '91's two Amy Yip blockbusters, its success largely attributed to the shapely presence of Japanese starlet Michiko Nishiwaki, one of the first actresses daring enough to take the plunge and move from mainstream features to one baring the dreaded Cat III symbol – a move which,

Before Naked Killers there was Killing in the Nude

femme on
femme in
The Love that
is Wrong

"Attention! Everyone must be decontaminate..."

— (Erotic Journey)

But if 1991 was a year of consolidation, '92 was the year the gloves came off completely and Eastern exploitation began to deliver in spades. Directed by and starring veteran 'Bruce Le' (a name lingering on from his earlier era as a Bruce Lee 'imitator') and starring Lily Li and Yuen Man, *Comfort Women* signalled the advent of a particularly sleazy trend in Hong Kong exploitation as the relaxation of curbs on sex and violence gave several producers the green light to combine both in movies where the sufferings and torments of scantily-clad babes became a principal focus of interest.

Not that this in itself was anything radically new. The Women In Prison/Prison Camp exploitationer has shown itself to be a hardy perennial the world over since the sixties, as any aficionado of *Caged Heat*, *Bare Behind Bars* or the quartet of *Ilsa* shockers will agree. *Man Behind The Sun* (1990) had established a benchmark in terms of pure gross vileness, but now it seemed the time was right to offer up lashings (usually literally) of misogyny to boot. There was a precedent for this type of feature: the Shaw Brothers had given us *Bamboo House of Dolls*, as straightforward a template of your typical gaoled women in peril flick as you could ask for. Swap jungle camp for urban slammer and you have such gems as Alan & Eric Films' *Women's Prison* (1988) and Paragon's *Jail House Eros* (1989). Any exploitation fan knows the drill: degradation and nastiness are our heroines' lot from start to finish when – these being, as ever, straight down the line morality tales – the tables are turned and the captives dispatch their tormentors in a vengeful orgy of retribution which naturally has the males in the audience contemplating the terrible fate awaiting any chap who mistreats a woman so awfully.

The proper way to eat
a stick of celery?
False Lady
Right:
Ghostly Love

oddly enough, garners little disapproval from the same movie establishment that draws the line at actors and directors moving in an opposite direction.

As 1991 drew to a close, the rise of this nascent genre was consolidated with steamy sagas such as *ABC Scandal*, *High School Student*, *High Class Model*, *Home For Intimate Ghosts*, *Tales of the Night* and *Ghost Love*, all titles in need of little or no explanation and all confirmation that this lewd and lascivious upstart genre was here to stay.

Comfort Women, however, is not wholly pitched at mysogynistic-level, possessing some intelligence in its storytelling. Based, as was *Man Behind The Sun* (with which it shares stylistic similarities), on true stories of Japanese cruelty to conquered populations in WW2 – in this case, the thousands of Korean women forced to serve as furlough 'entertainers' to the Emperor's troops – it focuses not only on the sexual and torturous privations of its female characters, but also on the strenuous efforts of the Japanese to ensure no one should know of their loathsome actions. As is pointed out at the film's end, only in 1991 did the Japanese acknowledge and apologize for their wartime actions. Whether this fact lends credibility to *Comfort Women* as a 'story-must-be-told' lest-we-forget document of history rather than a sleazy grindhouse number is up to you – however, I don't recall there being a gratuitous shower scene five minutes into *Judgement At Nuremberg*, do you?

If that sounds quibblesome, then at least Le's film has what might be called a context. Lar Kwok Hung's *Erotic Journey* (1993) proved that you didn't need to bother with that kind of nonsense in order to provide a healthy enough living for hack directors and a predominantly female cast willing to venture to that oh-so-familiar jungle-based prison camp set and go through the motions of yet another bargain-basement number. As cheap and not-very-cheerful exploitation goes, this stands comparison with even the most seedy Italian-lensed prison camp epic from the seventies: a plotline of utter incoherence, martial arts action of almost comic ineptitude and, naturally, the odd scene of harsh justice meted out to the unfortunate captives thrown in as a sad attempt to court notoriety.

Of course, the big Cat III phenomenon of '92 was the rise of Pauline Chan, who had capitalised on her success in the previous year's *Erotic Ghost Story III* to prove a popular box office draw in several floozie-focused sex dramas before the torrid and tawdry melodrama of *Escape From Brothel* made her name, another movie which, like *Comfort Women*, traded heavily on the women-in-(decidedly unpleasant)-peril schtick. However, this doesn't mean 1992 Cat III audiences only hungered for movies featuring damsels in untold distress. There were lighter

tso yung 左戒

Hong Kong starlet Tso Yung went to further her education in Australia when she was 15 years old. During her studies there she earned awards in several singing contests. By chance she caught the attention of a Hong Kong film worker who invited her to come back to Hong Kong and audition for a feature film being produced by Team Work Film Productions. The film she was cast in was the underrated *Women on the Run* (1993), a movie that will titillate any voyeur of high-kicking babes wearing micro-miniskirts and figure-hugging outfits. The camera angles alone of Tso Yung fighting on bamboo scaffolding will raise your temperature! It was this type of Cat III femme fatale film that producers didn't make enough of! To date this is the only film I believe she has completed.

chung ling 張睿玲

Chung Ling has made her reputation through eminent performances in adult movies. She has found recognition in movies like the steamy *Twenty Something* and is the other half of the battling babe duo in the (plenty of up-skirt-shot fighting scenes) *Women on the Run*.

filmography

1993	Women on the Run
1994	Twenty Something
	Victory

moments, most notably in the offering from Wong Tak Lung, the daffily randy *Dances With Snakes*, starring Hsu Meng Wah and Fan Li Chi. It's hard not to have a soft spot (or a somewhat lumpy one...) for this cheesily naff erotic fantasy comedy centred, with more than a few nods to *Sex and Zen*, on the involvement of a trio of pneumatic serpentesses with a lusty tavern owner who has, through overenthusiastic usage thereof, worn out his old chap. As a comedy it rarely ascends above the realm of the lowbrow, while as skin-flick fodder it comes across as affably naive and cack-handed, pleasingly devoid of any brutishness. *Dances With Snakes* represents the sillier side of Hong Kong sex-pictures, somewhat akin to British or German seventies 'erotica', where,

Lethal Panther

MARIA JO
MIYAMOTO YOKO

SIBELLE HUI
LAWRENCE NG

STEPHEN MILLER
MARK SCOTT
BRUCE STONE

Directed by GODFREY HO

Lethal Panther, aka Deadly China Dolls. Right: One of the scenes which suffered at the hands of the British censors

as including the most eye-popping knob-gag ever committed to celluloid – something to do with a hermit named 'Tim' and pretty much indescribable…

"The killer even broke his dick!!!"

— *(Naked Killer)*

Yet while the ladies were either carnally or torturously engaged in many of this year's Cat III product, a new sub-genre was fast-emerging, and *Naked Killer* marked its arrival with a blaze of sexy femme action that knocked audiences bandy and signalled the fact that perhaps the female of the species was deadlier than the male. Having shown that sexy babes toting meaningful weaponry was a recipe for equally-meaningful returns, *Naked Killer*'s progeny was not long in gestation. Of the spate of films which strove to mirror director Clarence Ford's full-on approach to carnal calamity capers, *Lethal Panther* aka *Deadly China Dolls* (1993) was perhaps one of the best. Helmed by Godfrey Ho, whose credits also include *Man Behind The Sun 2: Laboratory of the Devil* (1992), the sequel to the notorious T.F. Mous shocker and needing just as strong a stomach to view, *Lethal Panther/Deadly China Dolls* 'borrows' liberally from the plot of *The Killer*, but still manages to find a rollicking devastation-laden flow of its own regardless of budgetary constraints. Filmed, as is much of the ouvre of Ho, in the Philippines and starring local beauty, Maria Jo, plus Miyamoto Yoko and reliable action-femme Sibelle Hu, this movie proved that the femme fatale genre could be successful even on the most limited of budgets, a theory borne out by the fact that seemingly every director in Hong Kong has had their take on the genre, even Lee Tso Nam, best known as a kung fu filmmaker, weighing in the Moon Lee/Yukari Oshima vehicle, *Beauty Investigator* (1992), while the

however hard or strenuously the participants emoted and writhed, it still came across as naff, albeit in a wholesome and chucklesome way. If anything, it certainly deserves mention

same year brought us *Caged Beauties* aka *Fight For Love*, Yuan Ching Lee's Cat III action-fest set in a remote Thai guerrilla training camp and notable for a startling number of wet t-shirt scenes, if little else.

Intent upon pursuing the action-femme style, Joe Sui International cut down on the flair and raised the grittiness stakes with Yuen Kwai's tough *Women On The Run* (1992), an actioner about a female cop and junkie informant framed in a deadly drugs sting and undergoing all manner of grim ordeals before finally achieving payback in true Cat III fashion (i.e. the Bad Guy ends up singing soprano). Filmed partly on location in Canada, which lends the whole affair a more international and accomplished flavour, *Women On The Run* still shows its genre origins with more than a few gratuitous scenes and by the fact that its principle star, Yuen (*Operation Scorpio*) Jueng, often appears to be acting in another project entirely, not least in the film's martial arts scenes, which are well worth a look for fans of high-kicking action.

Exploring similar terrain, but to far greater cinematic effect, was an outstanding contribution from DLC Films, Cheung King Nin's *The Rapist Beckons* (1992), in which Chung Sok Fui plays traumatized rape survivor, Lily, a woman slowly but surely being pushed toward psychotic, vengeful rage by scumbag males and spiteful in-laws in a movie which takes the victim's point of view with such forceful consistency it almost nudges into the realms of social commentary – strong stuff for audiences in Hong Kong, where a male-dominated society still means issues such as this are more often swept under the carpet rather than aired in such a confrontational style. *The Rapist Beckons* packs a powerful punch,

They have the power… and the underwear to match! Power of Love

due not least to a strong performance from Chung Sok Fui and, a rarity where a good many Hong Kong films of this ilk are concerned, manages to communicate its agenda without losing sight of the fact that this is first and foremost a taut psychological action thriller. If watching it puts you in mind of Abel Ferrara's *Ms. 45: Angel of Vengeance* (1981), then all well and good. As with Ferrara's movie, *The Rapist Beckons* pulls off the tricky feat of stymieing any potential unsavoury fantasizing by male lowlifes among the audience with a swift and savage kick to predatory macho sensibilities liable to leave them wincing...

Above and right: *Sex and Zen*. Breaking new ground in erotic cinema

So 1992 proved a watershed year for foxy Cat III femmes and, after the category's somewhat confused origins, several distinct sub-genres were becoming established: the femme-fatale, flailing-fists and pistol-packing action pic; the medieval saucy sorcery shenanigans; the more questionable 'roughie', and the straightforward kit-off erotic potboiler. These categories within a category remain fairly consistent to date, although room still exists for invention and experimentation within the basic tenets of audience appeal.

An enticing nymph(o) in *Dances With Snakes*

"You have never make love with a woman..?"

— *(Power of Love)*

No less accomplished in terms of production values, but considerably easier on the eye, was *Pearls of the Orient* (1993), a second-hand *Dallas* with the shoulder pads off, whose lame wealthy family in sexy imbroglio storyline barely serves as anything more than a distracting backdrop for director/producer Chen Ching Te to dish up any number of nookie-crammed vignettes between the laboured exposition. Proof, if proof were needed, that anyone, from whatever culture they might herald, can still make a damn boring softcore sex movie.

Which is what, in essence, Chow Yeung and Leung Chi Hwa's *Power of Love* (1993) is all about. But whereas *Pearls of the Orient* attempted to ape the globally-accepted conventions as regards glossy sex movies, and failed abysmally as a consequence, this picture retains a skewed Hong Kong sensibility, thus providing the viewer with sufficient intrigue to prevent too much use of the fast-forward facility. Tai Yau Lay Choi and Loy Lee star in a convoluted tale of a housekeeper landed with a fortune in her lecherous ex-employer's will and the attempts by said lech's relatives to claim the old man's dough for themselves. How nymphomaniac female assassins and the erotic potential of a Hoover upright vacuum cleaner

become embroiled in this tale is something the reader will have to discover themselves. For an entertaining glimpse of what might be called a 'standard' Hong Kong sex movie, *Power of Love* is well worth a look. After all, as anyone who has ever sat through more than, say, a dozen softcore movies (even in the name of research!) will attest, a glazed-over ennui can soon set in as coupling follows coupling and the plinky-plonk synthesizer score begins to nag away at the viewer's synapses with all the

False Lady

top 10 asian babe cat III flicks

(TO CHECK OUT IN PRIVATE)

1 SEX AND ZEN
2 DEADLY CHINA DOLLS aka LETHAL PANTHER
3 WOMEN ON THE RUN
4 ROBOTRIX
5 EROTIC GHOST STORY
6 ESCAPE FROM BROTHEL
7 NAKED KILLER
8 A CHINESE TORTURE CHAMBER
9 PROFILES OF PLEASURE
10 the full frontal naked kung fu fight scene in NINJA THE FINAL DUEL

Alice Cheng bares all for Ninja the Final Duel

slightly higher than navel-level shows that perhaps Hong Kong moviemakers still haven't quite got the hang of this type of film – and all the better is it for that.

Then again, some filmmakers prefer to take a completely different approach, something evidenced in another 1993 offering, Lam Yee Hung's *My Better Half*, a picture which provides a welcome return for the portmanteau movie fondly-remembered by fans of late-sixties/early-seventies UK production company, Amicus (*The House That Dripped Blood, Asylum, Vault of Horror* etc.), in a trilogy mixing carnal carryings-on with heinous horror to bizarre effect. Best of all has to be Part Three, not only heavy on the gore, but also featuring the paranoid schizophrenic female character getting into an extraordinarily vivid verbal description of her sexual habits before an audience of bewildered cops. *My Better Half* is definitely something of an anomaly even for a Cat III feature and demonstrates an ever-closer relationship between the horror and sex genres in this field.

And where would sex and horror be without a good old-fashioned psycho stalker? Though the stalk 'n' slash seam was mined pretty much to exhaustion in western cinema courtesy of any number of movies with self-explanatory titles (*He Knows You're Alone, When A Stranger Calls*, and so on) and non-stellar casting, Cat III artisans detected signs

irritating persistence of Euro-Disco dreck. Anything that disrupts the monotony of a plotline no one involved can give a damn about as long as it somehow expedites further scenes of mattress-assault is welcomed as enthusiastically as a long-lost relative. These flicks can be as dull as any slab of earnest didactic materialism from the former Soviet Union. That *Power of Love* manages to engage your interest on a level

A busty group in Robotrix

III

of life in the thing yet and thus audiences were presented with a spate of pictures following this theme. Perhaps the blame should be laid squarely at the door of Simon Yam, whose eerie nut-on-the-brink screen presence defines the loony loner in any Hong Kong movie, regardless of category. Alas, whereas in *Bunman – The Untold Story* and *Love To Kill* Yam's twisted turn is showcased within an effective and stylishly rendered production, Hon Wei Tat's *Don't Stop My Crazy Love For You* (1993) suffers from a case of style over substance with Yam reduced to sleepwalking through a sub-standard performance as a deranged obsessive fixated on nightclub singer Kitty (played by Yung Hung) whose penchant for modelling her designer lingerie with the curtains open makes her a prime target for any weirdo with a high-powered telescope (guess who…) in a stultifying all-round disappointment which fails to even surpass the 1978 Lauren Hutton-starring telemovie *Someone Is Watching Me*, the basic premise of which Hon's picture heists wholesale.

Far more convincing an outing for Yam in mademoiselle-menacing-mode was a superior piece from Wong Jing's Workshop which reunited Yam with *Naked Killer* co-star Chingamy Yau. Directed by Wong Jing himself, *Raped By An Angel* (1993) resides in fairly conventional rape/revenge territory, with Yau the hapless apartment-dweller terrorized by a serial rapist and charts her struggle to gain justice first by legal means and, when that fails, via more direct action. If the rather ambivalent title suggests a heavy helping of misogyny, then those expecting the kind of exploitationer where we are subjected to prolonged brutal assaults as titillation for the jaded, albeit 'justified' by the rapist receiving their ultimate come-uppance, as in *I Spit On Your Grave* (1980) will be disappointed. Not that Wong Jing shies away from portraying the victims' terror – he doesn't – but there is no question at all with whom our sympathies are meant to lie.

Yet despite a well-constructed and acted story, *Raped By An Angel* somehow fails to gel convincingly, partially through the inclusion of an overly-long courtroom sequence which dissipates every bit of tension built up to that point. The much-discussed shocker dénouement is indeed the

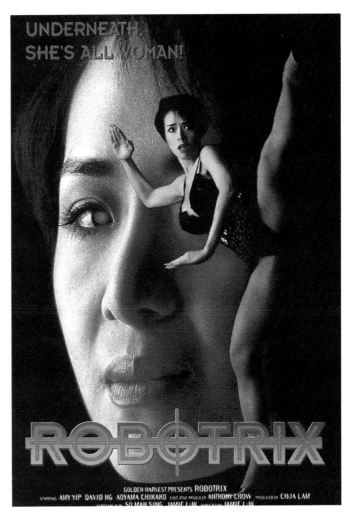

Devil Girl 18 video artwork

film's highlight, but it's a long time coming, time to reflect upon the fact that it seems almost as though the movie is too western in approach, too influenced by the conventions of Hollywood moviemaking and thus lacking those moments of jawdropping inspiration that are distinctively Hong Kong. Perhaps the idea was to capitalize on the burgeoning international reputation of post-*City Hunter* Chingamy Yau, yet the result is a curiously sterile affair, interest sustained mostly by a script which hammers home a message regarding the perils of AIDS and the importance of protected sex with an obsessive zeal.

"I desire to use many lusty instruments"

— (*A Chinese Torture Chamber*)

What *Raped By An Angel* and similar projects indicated was that by 1992-'93 Category III was being seen as an area which large-scale production companies could become involved in. It was no longer certain commercial suicide for producers to throw half-decent budgets and established performers at a Cat III project. Neither did it necessarily entail a wholesale descent into sleaze with every member of the cast required to cavort in the buff. What it did mean, though, was that directors were now given freer rein to produce action movies with a harder, more realistic, edge. These pictures naturally relied on sensationalism or shock to

attract the punters, but many of the Cat III films emerging from Hong Kong after 1992 display a gritty, no-holds-barred approach to matters such as social issues or politics while still respecting the basic tenets of the category, particularly in regard to sex and violence. *The Final Judgement* (1993), starring Simon Yam and Cecilia Yip, was one of the best examples of a sudden rush to put horrific true crime stories on the screen in the wake of the success of *Bunman*, while movies such as Scholar Film's *Psycho Cop* (1993), Johnny Lee's excellent and highly recommended *A Day Without Policemen* (1994) and Sing Po Production's *Big Circle Blues* (1994) further illustrate a leaning towards utilising the category as a means of taking Woo-esque bloodshed as a starting point from which things can only get nastier. And it's not just the boys who get the keys to the armoury, either – a good-looking gal who's nifty with an Uzi is now virtually de rigeur in this kind of movie, and if she hasn't wasted a brace of cops or bad guys (depending on her character's affiliation and/or disposition) then the viewer can count themselves cheated.

A move toward slicker, more accomplished Cat III productions does not signal an end to established seedier values. Flowers still bloom in the erotic garden and the shelves of Kowloon rental stores still bulge with any number of nookie-drenched potboilers of variable – to say the least – quality and all of

Left:

Erotic Journey

Far left:

Bunwoman: the

Untold Story?

My Better Half

them managing to get by without the pressures of multimillion dollar budgets hanging over their heads. Despite (or perhaps because of) this often-obvious shoestring approach, even this niche has thrown up the occasional surprise. *Ghost Love* (1991), a Lee Bo Tong produced cheapie lent weight by a battling appearance from Yukari Oshima, is the kind of thing we're talking about here – a bizarre plot involving a dead girl reincarnated as a beetle in order to gain revenge on the vice boss who caused her demise, Buddhist monks who materialize for no apparent reason, wholly gratuitous banana-eating and more – where, yes, the story exists as little more than something to pad the gaps between a succession of vigorous horizontal jogging scenes, but which, through its contrived, almost desperate, search for cohesion or even common sense becomes far more entertaining than the erotic abandonment itself. After all, when you've seen one sweaty encounter in a hotel room…

In fact, the softcore scene shows few signs of going into decline as yet, even if ideas aren't exactly in bountiful supply. *Nasty Spirit* (1994) revisits the *Dances With Snakes/Erotic Ghost Story* territory to fairly sexy, if pleasantly shoddy, effect, while even our old pal *Devil Girl 18* director Lam Wah Chun continues to hack out light-on-costume

Top: The girls relax after a busy day sucking the life out of virgins in Dances With Snakes
Above: Anthony Wong gets lucky in Erotic Ghost Story 2

numbers like the startling sex-cop-witchcraft-comedy-thriller *The Beauty's Evil Roses* (1994), a Thai-lensed S/M-heavy slice of hokum that occasionally manages to plumb previously uncharted reaches of insalubrity.

Yet it has been sleaze-king supremo Wong Jing who has made the most ripples upon the Cat III waters of late. His quickfire succession of startlingly OTT sex-shocks made 1994 the year the genre may have peaked in terms of just how far the parameters could be tested.

Girls just want to have fun boys – Sex and Zen

The Love That is Wrong

His trio of sex 'n' violence potboilers (*A Chinese Torture Chamber, Sex & The Emperor* and *Ancient Chinese Whorehouse*), and the

trouble they have caused, are examined in more detail elsewhere in the chapter, but there can be little doubt Wong's excesses have meant the genre is now being subjected to more scrutiny than ever. Not that it means the end of Category III, not by any means, for there is still many a chancer willing to invest in a production that's quick to complete, features plenty of carnal action, is guaranteed an audience and is cheap…

"All his neurotic system is damaged!"

— (Devil Girl 18)

There can be no doubt that without the talents of the likes of Amy Yip, Pauline Chan, Yung Hung et al this particular genre would have pretty much died at conception. New screen genres rely upon new screen icons in order to gain a toehold in the public imagination – where, for example, would seventies porno-chic have been without Sylvia Kristel of *Emmanuelle* fame? Likewise, Cat III's female stars (and their readiness to accept predominantly undraped roles) have created sufficient scandal and notoriety to maintain interest in one of the fastest-moving film industries in the world.

But whereas the major female players bring a name and box office appeal to attract meaningful talent to a few projects, the majority of movies in this area are independent, low-budget productions where the absence of big name talent can be overlooked as long as the finished product is sufficiently outrageous to justify its raunchy rating. It has to be borne in mind that in Hong Kong, as in most territories, the larger studios control the bulk of theatrical action, meaning for a great deal of films in this category, video constitutes the principal means of release. Allied to that is the fact that family features are still the chief staple of Hong Kong cinema and it becomes apparent that, far from being a liberating force in movie-making, Cat III can often be something of a ghetto, with only studio produced and financed pictures actually making it into first-run theatres. Cinemas devoted to more explicit entertainment exist, but these are more often than not small-scale, shabby places where the patrons don't take too kindly to any undue curiosity from passersby, a situation reminiscent of early 'adult' movie-houses in the States and the UK, frequented almost exclusively by the raincoat crowd, who know what they like and can live without a plot if need be. And with more and more of these films being released directly to video, it seems inevitable that even this crowd will eventually foresake the theatres for the more intimate interface provided by the VCR, with the consequence that the glut of shoddy, zero-budget Cat III fodder will only increase, making it even harder for a film to cross over to mainstream audiences.

However, there are a good many movies which simply do not merit widespread release. Take Toy Hong Films' *Devil Girl 18* (1992), for example, a cheap chunk of sexploitation which almost, but not quite, makes it into the 'so-inept-it's-fun' category, containing flubs, continuity gaffes, lousy acting and stock footage which has nothing whatsoever to do with the film aside from enabling the producers to topline a supposed 'cameo' by Yukari Oshima (*Shanghai Express*, *Story of Riki*, *Iron Angels*) in the hope of snaring a few hapless Oshima fans eager to see their idol get naked (and subsequently finding themselves most disappointed indeed). Even Edward D. Wood might have baulked at such a blatant stunt, but as hardened video-renters know, veracity is a word absent in the world of low-budget movie marketing – remember the post-*Basic Instinct* torrent of 'new' Sharon Stone product suddenly available at your local video emporium? Caveat emptor be always your watchword when wallowing in the murkier Cat III waters, as more than a few companies are not above tossing in a few moments of more risqué or gratuitously goresome action to spice up whatever utter clunker they've got on their hands if they think it might help it shift an extra unit or two – *Spiritual Love* (1992), *The Country*

Sex and Zen 2 – the Category III revival for '96?

Yung Hung goes a bit drastic in the do-it-yourself haircutting school – Sex and the Emperor

of Beauties (1982) and *Malevolent Mate* (1993) are but three examples of must-miss flicks to be going on with, but there are plenty of others besides, some so forgettable even the titles of the damn things elude me.

This sense of ghettoization is further reinforced when you consider the dearth of Cat III personnel managing to make the transition from this genre into other, more accepted, work. Where western stars and directors often used

Left: No, we didn't censor it! A typical pack image from a category III movie, minus offending nipples. Power of Love

exploitation as a means of getting their careers underway (George Lucas, Wes Craven and Jonathon Demme all worked in porno at the outset), its Eastern counterpart has yet to prove itself as fertile a breeding ground for screen luminaries of the future. Hong Kong actresses, for example, are nothing if not willing to go those extra few yards for a job – check out Margaret A Li expelling a mouthful of creepy-crawlies in Stephen C.K. Chan's *Centipede Horror* (1988), if you need confirmation – and if bevies of bodacious beauties in the buff figure heavily in a Cat III director's artistic vision then acres of underclad undulation he will have, so seemingly eager for work are actresses in search of that big break. But as yet mainstream cinema seems unwilling to permit said actresses to progress further, meaning that for many actors and directors Cat III is where their careers could begin and end.

With a genre barely a half-decade old such

an assertion may yet be proved wrong and we must not lose sight of the fact that for some, such as Simon Yam, perhaps the male equivalent of Amy Yip, this genre has brought them considerable acclaim. Yet Yam, as with Yip, has not found it easy to make the transition from exploitation to respectability, highlighting the oftentime sniffy opprobrium heaped upon the Cat III crowd by their wealthier and more powerful competitors.

The irony of this is that, alongside the work of Heroic Bloodshed exponents like John Woo and Ringo Lam, it is the more outlandish, extreme movies emerging from this genre which are responsible for an upsurge in interest in Hong Kong film unseen since the heyday of Bruce Lee. And if anyone is carrying the torch for the Hong Kong industry it has to be the Deadly China Dolls themselves. That this book exists at all is testament to that.

"*Your tits are too big, it made a man suffocate to death...*"

— *(Ancient Chinese Whorehouse)*

Yes, it's those gals again. Carrie and Chingamy just can't get enough of those provocative Naked Killer poses

One thing seems assured however, and that is that, whatever the immediate future might contain for Hong Kong cinema as a whole and Category III in particular, film fans from the US to the UK to Australia and all points beyond will continue to appreciate the delectable damsels of the Jade Screen and wait expectantly to see which starlet emerges from the confusion to be heralded as the latest Cat III sensation. There'll never be a shortage of surprises – just witness the sudden decision by (Loletta) Lee Lai Chun to start working in such movies, after twenty-five 'respectable' pictures. As long as Hong Kong adores beauty, the pageants will continue to bring to the fore fresh ingenues for the screen; Milk Ng (*Rock On Fire*) and Mondi Yau (*Romance Of The Vampires*) are but two new female stars to go from catwalk to camera in the past year or so.

Be it Chingamy Yau, Amy Yip, Pauline

Chan, Yung Hung or whoever, their movies will continue to find favour with those of us who have grown weary of the glossy yet ultimately vapid erotica which rolls off the production lines of American or European softcore hacks, each one a replica of the last. That's not to belittle the efforts of these hardy troupers – they strive to do their best – but what is lacking is that something extra you find only in a cinema which, though it may often take its cue from Tinseltown, cannot fail but overlay a character exclusively its own to whatever type of movie it produces, or even attempts to produce.

Category III has, in the space of only a few years, shown once more that exploitation or erotica does not have to be done by the numbers. Sure, this genre is not without the occasional turkey or two, but even the crummiest, zero-budget Hong Kong exploitationer will seldom lapse into the worst of all cinematic crimes: tedium. Why? Perhaps it is that we as westerners confronted by a cinema which has developed from a different historical perspective to our own, with its own mores, heritage and traits, fall prey to the fascination which cultural tourism always engenders.

Or maybe it is just that many westerners, whose knowledge and preconceptions of the Orient have been instilled in them by everything from *The World of Suzy Wong* to the *Kama Sutra* to lurid tales of sordid goings-on down the Patpong Road, have an in-built response mechanism when contemplating Eastern sexuality.

Or perhaps it is that Hong Kong cinema is always alive with a zest for moviemaking rarely found among our own output. Allied to which is a desire – almost a compulsion – to deliver something novel, something the audience is completely unprepared for. Cat III has opened up new directions in the Hong Kong scene, new avenues to explore and filmmakers are eager and enthusiastic to see just where these paths will lead. Even the sex movie, formerly as stale a genre as you could imagine, has been re-invigorated and transformed into a genre capable of providing the heady, sexy – even downright silly – erotic escapism previously only extent in the work of maverick auteurs like Joe Sarno, Stephen Sayadian or Russ Meyer (imagine him remaking *Naked Killer*!). Furthermore,

whereas western erotica is primarily the domain of actresses with – to put it kindly – a limited range, Hong Kong directors can call upon foxy femmes more than capable of handling whatever demands the latest script throws at them, be it action in the form of frenzied and exhausting martial arts and gunplay, or complex and dangerous stunt-work, or a spot of undraped libidinous lust played either for sensual intensity or merely for cheap laffs. Lord, you can even give some of them a serious script and they won't let you down..!

Then again, perhaps it is something far less tangible, far more instinctive – perhaps it is that here we have found a form of cinema that delivers that all-important knockout blow to our aesthetic sensibilities and leaves us reeling, dazed and brimming with the delight each and every movie fan feels upon watching something completely different.

Above:
Category III
exploitation for 1996 –
Horrible High Heels

A blast from the past –
Blood Ritual

AMY YIP

葉子楣

"EVERY
MALE
FEMME
FATALE
FAN'S
DREAM"

–Amy Yip in
Sex and Zen

'wow! what busts!'

amy yip

text:
Howard Lake

Let's be upfront about this...

The influence of buxom Amy Yip (aka Yip Chi Mei) on the popularisation of the Cat III movie cannot be underestimated. Indeed, any discussion of the merits or otherwise of these films will invariably return to the actress who has been to Hong Kong what Monroe and Mansfield were to Hollywood in the fifties and Bardot was to French cinema in the sixties – a starlet who is more than simply sexy, but whose sexual presence transcends a mere love affair with the camera to become a phenomenon all its own. Certainly, she is the actress with whom (male, testosteronally-fuelled) western audiences have swiftly grown infatuated and in Hong Kong itself very few men would declare anything but undying affection from the waist down, one notable exception being Jackie Chan who declared her 'the ugliest woman I've ever seen' (from which we can only assume his stunt mishap during *Project A* did more damage to his noggin than first

Come...

...sink...

...with me

How to give a toe
an erection?
Sex and Zen

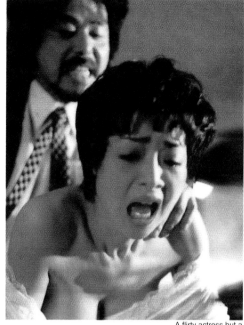

assumed). Brickbats from Jackie notwithstanding, Amy Yip definitely brings an alluring charisma and sexy charm to any film in which she appears.

Born on June 10, 1965 and educated at Kau Kam English College, Amy Yip was determined to succeed in the entertainment industry, enrolling in stage classes and rapidly moving into television with Hong Kong network ATV. A modest progression of daytime shows and supporting roles failed to provide job and career satisfaction and by 1987 she had signed her first contract with Golden Harvest. After a succession of minor roles in lightweight fluff such as *The Inspector Wears a Skirt 2* (1989) and *My Neighbours Are Phantoms* (1990), her first part of any substance came with a now infamous scene as a hooker in *Blue Jean Monster* (1990) where her soon-to-be-famous busty bits are given a fearful squeeze by a zombie, resulting in a somewhat tasteless shower of mother's milk and a subsequent deflation of said appendages.

The irony of that, erm, 'defining' movie moment should not be ignored, for Yip's bits – 35" since you asked – are big news in Hong Kong, debate as to the authenticity of her pectoral achievement always a tasty subject for gossip columnists and film fans (particularly female fans) alike. That in her screen career to date she has contrived to avoid showing completely all (earning yet another nickname, 'Yip Tease' in

the process) should give you one clue.

While Amy has posed for Chinese *Penthouse* and *Playboy*, she has scrupulously shunned full-on flauntage; even a book of erotic model shots, *Limited Sexy Picture*, was cunningly contrived to keep fans guessing.

The author will admit that, yes, it does seem overly prurient to dwell upon such a matter, but, whereas cosmetic enhancement of an actress'

Amy Yip proves a real handful in Robotrix

embonpointment is par for the course (cynics would say compulsory) in Hollywood, it is still a rarity in the Hong Kong movie world and therefore as juicy a topic for frenzied tabloid speculation as any new picture of Pamela Anderson in a swimsuit would be over here. Even when she retired from the screen, the subject remained a hot item. As recently as summer 1995 tabloid headlines screamed: Taiwan Rumour: Broken Tits! alongside a piece claiming Amy's augmented tributes had sprung a leak.

Leaving, with some relief, the matter aside for the time being, the Cat III movies of Amy Yip act in many ways as the benchmark by which all others should be judged. Her films have varied widly, veering from straightforward erotic potboilers to bizarre sex-comedies to sci-fi action, the only constant being that at some point or other the script will call for her to lose her laundry and engage in a sizeable chunk of sultry writhing, and for her to be the butt of the kind of knocker-gag even Benny Hill might discard as a teensy bit crass (more often than not Yip's character will possess a nomenclature as subtle as 'Chesty')… Cat III is nothing if not unflinchingly lowbrow when it comes to anatomical humour.

However, this should not be taken as meaning Cat III's leading lust-object is not a competent actress. To western audiences her screen presence is an intriguing mix of airhead and feisty femme, witnessed to best effect in Jamie Luk's *Robotrix* (1991), an early – and reasonably successful – entry in the Cat III stakes from Golden Harvest. This sexy *Robocop*-influenced sci-fi actioner cast Yip alongside comely co-stars Hsu Hsiao Dan and Aoyama Chikako as an android with an urge to discover what being 'truly human' is all about. No prizes for guessing what this might entail, but when not going undercover at a brothel (all vital to the plot, honest), Yip shows herself more than capable of handling the high-kicking rough stuff. She's no Angela Mao Ying, but if nothing else proves her talents extend beyond her double-D decolletage.

The HK$6m box office achieved by *Robotrix* convinced Golden Harvest there was gold in them thar thrills and with almost indecent haste shooting commenced, under the direction of Michael (*Long Arm of the*

How does she manage to keep her balance? I hear you cry

Sex and Zen. Tie me up...

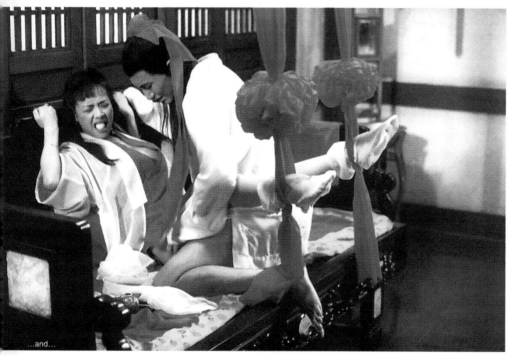

...and...

...tie me down

Law 2) Mak, on what was to become the Cat III success story and the film which finally elevated the genre to the status of serious box office contender: *Sex and Zen* (1991).

The returns were something else: an awesome HK$18.5m upon release, plus the added kudos of a six-week chart-topping run in, of all places, Italy. Then again, *Sex and Zen* was something else, too. Adapted, to use the term loosely, from *Yu Pu Tuan*, a major 17th Century Ming Dynasty novel, *Sex and Zen* was a deliriously insane rollercoaster ride through the erotic misadventures of randy scholar Sheng (Lawrence Ng), determined to disprove the Buddhist credo of abstinence. Marriage to Nina (Yip) would seem to be a step in the right direction. But, feeling he lacks the, er, necessary equipment Sheng heads for the local stables in search of a suitable equine donor for a penis transplant. At this point, Cat III comes into its own and we are in the realms of sheer confounded amazement of the kind touched upon at the beginning of this chapter. And once lift-off is achieved a return to anything akin to normality is a long time coming.

But is it actually erotic? This, of course, depends upon what turns you on, but examined in terms of 'conventional' erotica *Sex and Zen*, like a good many other Cat III sex films, conforms to the standard tenets of the genre – artfully-lensed, vaseline-tinted couplings accompanied by seductive music; the expected whimperings of ecstacy from

the ever-grateful female – and a good many interludes would not seem out of place in the works of European or American softcore directors such as Tinto Brass, Just Jaeckin or Zalman King (indeed, veteran Italian hack Joe D'Amato was sufficiently inspired by *Sex and Zen* to rip it off several times over in his 1993 flicks *The Dream of the Red Room, Sex & Chinese Food* and *Chinese Kamasutra* – under the pseudonym Robert Yip). Yet, although near-explicit bonking is often the whole point of some Cat III flicks, in *Sex and Zen* the act itself is often the starting point for things to become genuinely outrageous – either in terms of stunningly sexist brutality or almost ludicrous kinkiness – in a way which suggests that for Mak, and for other directors in the field, the pleasure is in constructing scenes completely different from anything you've seen before. Sit through a clutch of movies and you'll soon understand the way some Cat III film makers enjoy subverting your expectations. In *Sex and Zen* there's everything from sex underwater to two women making intriguing use of a flute to a rather nasty piece of rough stuff to a pyschedelic lesbian S&M bondage scene (the author confesses he could be a tad hazy on that last one), while other movies up the strangeness quotient even further with such delights as exploding

Amy Yip and friend consider a threesome in Erotic Ghost Story

Top: Amy is busting out all over!

Right: A sultry Amy Yip in Sex and Zen

Top right: Amy poses for the camera in a publicity shot for Robotrix

Middle: The Inspector Wears a Size 34DD… Robotrix

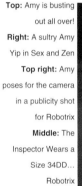

Amy easily stands out from an all-star crowd in Raid on Royal Casino Marine

penises, high-speed mid-air bonking (A Chinese Torture Chamber), six-foot high erections and naked oil wrestling (Dances With Snakes) and that old standby, discovering the allure of the bathroom loofah (Ghostly Love). From this bizarre, often surreal approach to its subject matter comes much of the appeal of Cat III sex movies. Whereas western examples of the genre tend toward an evenness of tone, one stylized and choreographed copulation after another, Cat III leans more toward the philosophy of something for everyone and so there's nothing unusual in a rape scene, say, abruptly veering off into comedic farce, or the plot of a movie being only capable of resolution by two pure-in-heart virgins making love – a device which crops up in a remarkable number of films for some odd reason…

Neither is there anything amiss in the idea of a female vampire required to 'suck the sperm and devour the essence' of a hundred male virgins, a premise which drove the plot of Ghostly Vixen (1990), the movie that launched Yip to Hong Kong stardom, yet which remained largely undiscovered until Robotrix and Sex and Zen catapulted her to international fame.

However, once Yip was firmly installed as the Number One babe in the minds of Cat III audiences she wasted no time in consolidating her position. Her career to date includes an exhausting eighteen films in four years, some of which [*Vampire Kids* (1989), *Jail House Eros* (1989)] are instantly forgettable and others, like *To Be Number One* (1992), *Requital* (1992) and *China Dolls* (1993) which allow Yip to extend her skills to a commendable degree. The latter is especially worth viewing, a gritty saga of a young mum forced into life as a Macau call-girl, in which Yip proves herself as adept at handling a downbeat gloomy script as she is with any of the mattress-actioners with which she made her name.

At the time of writing, though, Yip's screen activities would appear to be on more or less permenant hold. Even in retirement, however, the star is a source of much discussion in Hong Kong, as well as generating plenty of juicy gossip for fans to mull over: she's fed up with pressure from Triads; her bank manager boyfriend defrauded his employer to finance her extravagant lifestyle, and so on.

A singing career launched in 1991 began well, with earnings in the region of about HK$10m being bandied. By now she had left Hong Kong for Taiwan and, under manager Wu Dun's supervision, was playing venues as far-flung as Vegas and drawing in huge crowds, most of whom, it must be noted, had come more to gaze at Amy's figure in an array of eye-popping stage outfits than to marvel at her vocal ability. CDs followed, selling well, but by 1993 Yip had entered a serious relationship with a wealthy doctor and all but vanished from the Asian entertainment scene. Reports suggested she had retreated into comfort paid for by some astute property investments, but it wasn't until tabloid gossips began claiming the starlet's inertia had gained her tonnage of Liz Taylor-esque proportions that a severely miffed Ms. Yip reappeared – but only after a frenzied fitness regime had ensured the restoration of her earlier physiognomical splendour. This, however, has not heralded a return to the screen or the stage and it would appear for now that her career is to, all intents and purposes, a done deal... although certainly not forgotten.

AMY-ography
Amy Yip / Yip Chi Mai

葉子楣

1989	Vampire Kids
	Jail House Eros aka Jail House Girls
	Mr Canton and Lady Rose aka Miracles
	To Spy With Love
	The Inspector Wears a Skirt
1990	My Neighbours are Phantoms
	Blue Jean Monster
	Ghostly Vixen
	Erotic Ghost Story
	Erotic Ghost Story 2
	Skinned Ghost
	The Inspector Wears a Skirt 2
1991	Robotrix
	Sex and Zen
	Easy Money
	Look Out Officer
	The Great Pretender
	Lethal Contact
	Underground Judgement
	Raid on Royal Casino Marine
	Ghost Fever
	Legend of the Dragon
1992	To Be Number One
	Requital
	Queen of the Underworld
	Magnificent Scoundrels
	Stooges in Hong Kong
1993	China Dolls
	Lucky Way

Amy and crew are on the scene for Robotrix

CHINGAMY YAU

邱淑貞

Chingamy Yau poses with Jaqueline Ng for a raunchy publicity shot for Naked Killer 2 aka Raped by an Angel

from sex kitten to superstar
chingamy yau

**text:
Howard Lake**

Chingamy Yau – I'm not so good...

I'm not so bad...

Of all the starlets to make their name in the often-seamy world of Category III movies, Chingamy Yau (Yau Suk Ching) is probably the babe most male viewers would feel secure taking home to meet the family. It makes sense: Amy Yip's decolletage might dazzle dad, and mum might get funny ideas about what Pauline Chan did for a living, but Chingamy..? You get the feeling the folks might just warm to her.

...but I can definitely get ugly!

Chingamy Yau and Simon Yam get mad in Dangerous Couple

Inset: Chingamy poses for the camera

God of Gamblers 2

Of course, were the obligatory drunken uncle the family's all embarrassed about to show up and attempt to tickle her

tush over the vol-au-vents, chances are your intended might show a different aspect to her character, as lecherous in-law violently interfaces with the trifle courtesy of a well-aimed stiletto heel to the grollies. Therein resides the charm of Chingamy Yau's screen persona: scrummily wholesome but possessed of considerable reserves of feistiness if needs be.

Nowhere better is this illustrated than in, of course, *Naked Killer*. But as integral an aspect in the worldwide popularisation of Asian actresses and Category III movies as this classic is, *Naked Killer* appears to be just one stop in the career of an actress with her sights determinedly set on the top.

Whatever her ultimate destination, Yau couldn't have had a much better start in terms of timing. Perhaps she was fortunate to come to the notice of Hong Kong's exploitation king, Wong Jing, just as his particular brand of carnage and carnality was doing a beat-

王晶

'em-up of Mike Tyson magnitude on local box offices. Certainly a sussed cookie like Wong wasn't slow to see that this slender yet curvaceous model with the expressive eyes and underpant-melting smile had potential in spades. After finding her filmic feet in the zany 1991 ghost comedy *My Neighbours Are Phantoms* (alongside Amy Yip, no less) and a clutch of unremarkable thrillers (*She Starts the Fire*, *Deadly Dream Woman* and *Casino Tycoon*), Wong pitched her into *Naked Killer* to instant acclaim from critics and fans alike.

Yau and Wong were quick to cash in on their success. An historical action pic, *Legend of the Liquid Sword*, swiftly followed and while Chingamy didn't disgrace herself in a fairly minor role, the movie itself was hardly anything to write home about. A return to a darker theme proved a better bet and *Raped by an Angel* (sometimes known as *Naked Killer 2* – but don't be fooled), a hard boiled rape/revenge drama co-starring Simon Yam, has become one of Yau's best-known features. As the outraged heroine who ultimately gives rapist Yam his bloody come-uppance, Yau once again showed a depth to her performance which revealed her to be more than mere onscreen ornamentation.

Not a lass to rest on her laurels, Chingamy was soon back in front of Wong Jing's cameras for Lau Wei Keung's pleasantly brutal *All New Human Skin Lanterns*, a revamping of the Shaw Brothers 1982 shocker. A teaming up with major names like Samo Hung and Jet Lee followed in *Kung Fu Cult Master* (1993), a surreal martial arts fantasy which proved Yau was ready for the big time.

And co-stars don't come much more bigtime than Jackie Chan, with whom Yau was cast in 1993's *City Hunter*. Though produced by the giant Golden Harvest, Wong Jing was again at the helm and he made certain his protegée garnered as much time alongside the main man as possible. The move paid off as Yau's performance as the pulchritudinous PI picked up many a rave and cemented her status as an actress worth watching – and

not exclusively because her mini-skirts appeared to have been designed by someone on a zealous mission to reduce the movie's costume budget.

1994 brought a reunion with Jet Lee in *New Legend Of Shaolin*, a generally

Chingamy goes Manga-in-Motion!
Above: City Hunter
Left: Future Cops

Chingamy Wow!!! A series of glamourous shots for My Birthday Cake

well-received retread of a familiar martial arts saga, but Chingamy's part was a comparatively minor one compared to the starring role she landed in Chin Man Kei's *1941: Hong Kong on Fire*, a tough and often

shocking drama that paired Chingamy with Cecilia Yip as sisters enduring the privations of Japanese occupation during World War II. Here, perhaps for the first time, Yau had an opportunity to carry an entire picture on her own and she accepted the challenge with relish, sweeping the plaudits in a well-made and credible story that combines moments of light-hearted comedy with some truly harrowing scenes.

Yau's versatility has propelled her close to the top bracket of Hong Kong movie stars as she has successfully escaped the Category III niche in which she made her name and moved on to work of genuine substance such as supporting hyperstars Chow Yun Fat and Tony Leung in 1995's *God of Gamblers 2* (aka *Return of God of Gamblers*) or the same year's *My Birthday Cake*. Not only do her screen parts pack extra punch nowadays, so does her earning power – a 1995 survey placed her joint fifteenth in the Hong Kong entertainers' pay league with a booty estimated in the region of HK$5m... and rising.

Do we really need to tell you? Naked Killer

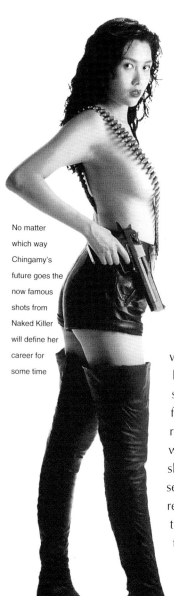

No matter which way Chingamy's future goes the now famous shots from Naked Killer will define her career for some time

Deadly Dream Woman

Return (aka *Devil 666*), a Hong Kong version of the Hollywood blockbuster, *Seven* – and has given magazine interviews that suggest a spirited attempt to finally leave her 'bad girl' image behind for good, painting a picture of an offscreen life of almost cloying wholesomeness. At this rate, who knows? Mum and dad could be rolling out the red carpet before long and certain uncles will most definitely not be invited...

With such box office clout and a huge legion of fans, it could well be that Chingamy Yau becomes the first actress to successfully make the transition from Category III sex kitten to respectable thespian status, though whether she will ever completely shed her siren image remains to be seen – as long as *Naked Killer* retains its popularity one suspects those publicity shots will continue to define her image for some time to come. These days Yau can certainly be more selective in her choice of screen work – she began 1996 alongside Donnie Yen in *Satan's*

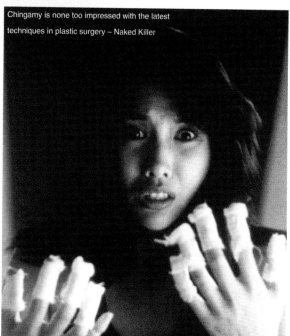

Chingamy is none too impressed with the latest techniques in plastic surgery – Naked Killer

Chingamy rides the dragon in Lover of the Last Empress

CHING-ography

Chingamy Yau / Yau Suk Ching

邱淑貞

1988	The Crazy Companies
	Mr Possessed
	How to Pick
	The Crazy
	Companies 2
1989	They Came to
	Rob Hong Kong
	Mister Fortune
	Ghost Busting
	Romancing the Star 3
1990	Happy Together
1991	Tricky Brains
	My Neighbours Are Phantoms
	Money Maker
	Lee Rock
	Lee Rock 2
1992	School Commandos
	Casino Tycoon
	Casino Tycoon 2
	Royal Tramp
	Royal Tramp 2
	Naked Killer
	Deadly Dream Woman
	Truant Heroes
	She Starts the Fire
	Psycho Cop (TV)
1993	Millionaire Cop
	City Hunter
	Legend of the Liquid Sword
	Raped by an Angel aka Naked Killer 2
	Holy Weapon
	Future Cops
	Boys Are Easy
	Ghost Lantern
	Kung Fu Cult Master

1994	New Legend of Shaolin
	The Modern Love
	Return to a Better Tomorrow
	1941: Hong Kong on Fire
1995	Lover of the Last Empress
	My Birthday Cake
	Dangerous Couple
	God of Gamblers 2
	aka Return of the God of Gamblers
	Saint of Gamblers
	High Risk
1996	Satan Returns aka Devil 666
	Street Angel

She'll be your birthday cake!!

CARRIE NG

吳家麗

born to thrill

carrie ng

It's scenes like this that has made Naked Killer the number one femme fatale film in the UK – and it's uncut!

A Naked Killer, apart from the hat maybe....

text:
Howard Lake

Jackie Chan adopts his own Naked Killer pose with Carrie

Carrie Ng shoots to kill in Crystal Hunt

If **Naked Killer**
was the accelerant which sparked Chingamy Yau's career, then in a similar, if not quite as dramatic, way Clarence Ford's classic also finally brought her co-star, Carrie Ng, the acclaim she rightly deserves.

In many respects, the two actresses paths couldn't be more different. For while Yau's ascent to big-name hoopla and the attendant

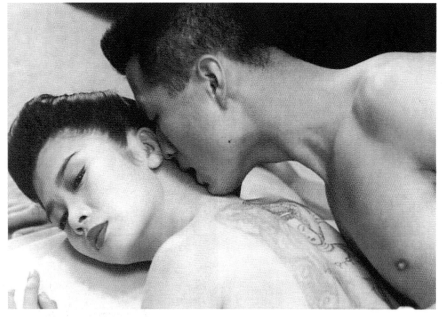

moolah that brings has been a rapid one, Carrie Ng (Ng Kar Lee) has followed a path towards success that displays an indomitable and dogged determination, often in the face of treatment from producers and directors alike that might have had lesser actresses throwing it in long ago.

She's a fighter. Of that there can be no doubt. Born in Kowloon in 1963, Carrie, like countless Hong Kong youngsters, dreamed of screen stardom from an early age. In interviews she has told of a modest upbringing, of being a teenager of decided awkwardness and gawky looks. Yet, as she matured and shed her youthful ungainliness she determined to follow through her dreams of a career in the entertainment industry. After completing school, she landed a place at the drama academy run by TVB, the biggest television network in Hong Kong. Her parents were reportedly less than thrilled by their daughter's choice of vocation but, undeterred, Carrie pressed on and before long had made her small-screen debut.

If Carrie had been anticipating overnight elevation to the dizzying heights of stardom she was to be disappointed. TV bigwigs considered her

Top: Oh lucky man, whispering sweet nothings in a tatooed Carrie's ear...

Middle: Carrie gets frisky with her sidekick in Naked Killer

Bottom: Carrie attempts to play footsie with a poolside mate

Right: Ouch! One in the head for one of Carrie's victims in Naked Killer

appearance too outré for leading lady parts and she soon found herself languishing in typecasting hell, saddled with a welter of scheming jezebel/loose woman rôles and barely allowed more than a few lines before receiving her properly moral come-uppance. Through sheer bloody-mindedness, she persevered until her share of dialogue actually amounted to a page or two, but still Carrie Ng remained, in the eyes of her overlords at least, the vampish vixen who added allure but wasn't ever taken seriously as an actress.

Which was why, in 1987, Carrie made the bold move of swapping the boob tube for the Jade Screen. After two flicks (and parts) of little consequence, her new career received a considerable boost when she played against Chow Yun Fat in Ringo Lam's *City On Fire*, a movie which was to be something of a watershed in the rise of the Heroic Bloodshed genre (and in the rise of a certain Mr. Tarantino of Los Angeles, for that matter). It wasn't easy for Carrie to make a mark amidst the double-pistolled, high-ordnance mayhem, but she must have done something right as thereafter the phone began ringing chez Ng with satisfying regularity.

Fair enough, the majority of parts on offer were of the decorative variety, but even in hokum like the Pauline Chan vehicle *Girls Without Tomorrow* or *Fury* or *He Who Chases After The Wind* (all 1988), Carrie was able to show herself capable of thesping with the best – and worst. The Tsui Hark-produced *Gunmen* (1989), starring Tony Leung, brought her a modicum of attention as the standout actress in a middling movie, as did her gritty performance in the Women In Prison drama *The First Time Is The Last Time* (1989), but despite an ever-burgeoning profile the typecasting she'd encountered in television persisted.

Ever the fighter, Carrie struggled womanfully to shuck the shackles of slutdom, taking roles in comedies like *A Fishy Story* (1989) and the Samo Hung-starrer *Skinny Tiger, Fatty Dragon* (1990), while also wallowing in real bottom-of-the-barrel trash like the ultra-sleazy *Hero Dream* (1992), but while critical opinion was on the whole encouraging, Ng was still looking for the movie that would elevate her above the status of also-ran. A succession of parts in flicks as

Top: Carrie Ng with Andy Lau in Days of Tomorrow

Middle: Again with Andy in Gun 'N' Rose

Bottom: Once again with Andy in The First Time is the Last Time

Carrie Ng poses with Jackie Chan

Days of Tomorrow

(1991), the movie that made Amy Yip a star, showcased Carrie's talents in a low-key light. There must have been times she thought her career was destined to be that of a supporting player, never the star.

1992 was the year everything changed as, in true Knight In Shining Armour fashion, producer Wong Jing cast Carrie in *Naked Killer*, playing the slinky Sapphic rub-out artist Princess. Despite, or perhaps because of, a strong line-up of co-stars (Chingamy Yau, Simon Yam), Ng made sure this time that she wasn't going to be upstaged. In this she was completely successful and, thereafter, no one but no one was going to regard Carrie Ng as an actress who showed purely to make up the numbers.

If 1992 and *Naked Killer* thrust Carrie into the limelight, then the following year saw her up the brightness to supernova qualities as she teamed up once again with *Naked Killer* helmer Clarence Ford for the true crime thriller *Remains Of A Woman*. At face value it appeared to be little more than a typical Cat III flick, albeit with a scad of style, and certainly local audiences weren't overly enamoured of the movie upon release. But the film was a colossal hit in Taiwan and it could have been this which led to the sensational news that its leading actress was nominated for Best Actress at that year's Golden Horse Awards (the Hong Kong equivalent of the Oscars) – sensational as this was the first time the Cat III genre had even been acknowledged by the mainstream of Hong Kong cinema.

Even so, Carrie was one hell of an outsider, so when the incredible occurred and the announcement was made that Ng had scooped the top prize, the response was remarkable. Carrie herself was almost too overcome to make her acceptance speech and the reverberations of her achievement were to linger for months. In terms of Carrie's career, she had finally achieved the goal for which she had battled so long, the ultimate accolade, but she had no intention of stopping there. A hard-hitting actionfest, *Black Panther Warriors* (1993), continued her association with director Clarence Ford to

Black Panther
Warriors

diverse as the narco-actioner *Dragon Fighter* (1990), gang-war shoot-em-up *Blood Stained Tradewinds* (1990) and the martial arts bonesplitter *Dragon From Russia* (1990) proved that not only could Carrie Ng look the business but that she was also capable of dishing out the destruction herself, but the huge hit she craved remained elusive. Even a part in the Cat III breakthrough *Sex & Zen*

good effect, consolidating her position as one of the most sought-after actresses in Hong Kong cinema.

The kudos of her Golden Horse award means that Carrie no longer has to take any rôle she's offered, yet she has not in any way disassociated herself from the tough, in-yer-face movies that made her name. The genre seems to suit her – and her many fans – just fine. Post-*Remains...* she has featured in a number of films which flirt with exploitation without veering too close to Cat III carnality. *Story Of Pei-Li* (1993) was a low-key drama centred around an escort agency, while titles like *Armed Policewoman* and *Passion Unbound* (1995) require little explanation. More recent films have seen Ms. Ng up the ante in the sexuality stakes with *Evil Instinct* (1996) a revamp (no pun intended) of *Basic Instinct*. One glance at the film's poster – Carrie wearing nothing but a ten-foot python – will tell you that this femme knows what her audiences like.

And it's an army of fans that's steadily increasing, as Western audiences discover the offbeat allure of Carrie Ng, inspired primarily by the video release of *Naked Killer*. As more of her pictures make it to the UK and beyond, we can be sure that Carrie Ng will become perhaps one of the icons of the Asian Babe genre. It's something she deserves...after all, few actresses have worked as hard as she to make it all the way to the very top.

CARRIE-ography
Carrie Ng / Ng Kar Lee

吳家麗

1987	To Err is Humane		
	I'm Okay, You're Okay		
	City on Fire		
1988	Girls Without Tomorrow		
	Fury		
	He Who Chases After the Wind		
	Mistaken Identity	1992	The Incorruptibles
1989	Gunmen		Misty
	A Fishy Story		Angel Terminators
	Fight to Survive	1993	Days of Tomorrow
	The Nobles		Black Panther Warriors
	Fire Phoenix		Remains of a Woman
	The First Time is the Last Time		Thrilling Story
	Missing Man		Young Wiseley
1990	Blood Stained Trade Winds		Mission of Justice
	Dragon From Russia		Never Ending Love
	Dragon Fighter		The Story of Pei-Li
	Queen's Bench 3		Sentenced to Hang
	Forsaken Cop		C'est la Vie Mon Cherie
	Skinny Tiger, Fatty Dragon	1994	Rock 'N' Roll Cop
	Family Day	1995	Armed Police Woman
1991	Au Revoir Mon Amour		Passion Unbound
	Sex and Zen		Candlelight Woman
	Weakness of Man	1996	Evil Instinct
	A Rascal's Tale		Thunder Cop
	The Ultimate Vampire		
1992	Best of the Best		
	Mountain Warriors		
	My Americanised Wife		
	Gun 'N' Rose		
	Justice My Foot		
	Sex and Curse		
	Taking Manhattan		
	Changing Partners		
	Naked Killer		
	Angel Hunter		
	Call Girl '92		
	Crystal Hunt		
	Cheetah on Fire		
	Hero Dream		
	Twilight in the Forbidden City		

PAULINE CHAN

陳寶蓮

"YOUNG AND DANGEROUS"

'I want to see a live show tonight...'

A casual but cute Pauline Chan

pauline chan

'...but I really want to sing!'

text:
Howard Lake

Of **1992's** big Category III hits, one movie in particular garned an inordinate amount of attention. Directed by Johnny Mak, the flick was a particularly vivid venture into the realms of celluloid sleaze and featured privations inflicted upon its two female

the essential guide to deadly china dolls • **247**

Escape From Brothel.
Pauline Chan's
finest hour?

Two's company three's a crowd – a scene cut by British Censors – Escape From Brothel

Erotic Ghost Story 3

flurries of scissor-wielding by the UK's own BBFC when released on video three years later). It was exploitation at its most relentless and nasty. The movie was *Escape From Brothel.*

Backed by the sizeable Ocean Shores concern, this relentlessly grim tale of Hung sold into Happy Valley hookerdom to settle her husband's gambling debts struck a HK$6m chord with audiences won over by extremely explicit – even by Cat III standards – sex scenes combined with several moments of jawdropping unpleasantitude, in which

protagonists that were strong stuff by anyone's standards (indeed, it caused more than a few

electrocution and a baseball bat figure heavily, further indicating a demand for pictures to provide more raw meat upon which audiences could chew.

A substantial portion of the picture's success would have to be attributed to its leading ladies, Rene Murakami and, especially, the actress portraying the luckless Hung, Pauline Chan. Born in Shanghai in 1975, Chan (aka Chan Bo Lin) was already shaping up to be one of Hong Kong's hottest Cat III phenomena. Her largely-unclothed role in *Erotic Ghost Story 3* (1991), in which she displayed admirable commitment to the many and varied lubricious scenes so vital to the plot, had ensured a sizeable following for this former beauty pageant contestant and by the time she quit movies to pursue a singing career in '93, interest was at a high for this leggy starlet, with endless gossip (a sure sign of success) about her allegedly profligate ways with money filling the tabloids and magazines – including the accusation that she was having a house-extension planned to accomodate her ever-expanding wardrobe!

One has to say this is a success created almost solely on her looks, for even a cursory examination of the twenty-odd movies in her canon reveals very little in the way of quality, although *Girls From China*, *Ladies From Shanghai* and *Girls Without Tomorrow* (all 1992) are entertaining enough sexy potboilers of small consequence in which Chan plays the whorish roles she was burdened with throughout her career (see also: 1992's *A Wild Party* and *Behind The Pink Door*) with commendable gusto, despite reproducing roles with which she was already overly-familiar. Wong Chi's *Girls Without Tomorrow* deserves special mention for Chan's beyond-the-call-of-duty part of a hooker catering to kinky clients, where as well as being immured in any amount of PVC and rubberwear, she's even smeared in ketchup and milk (!) prior to being whipped by a sadistic Japanese client. And they said the movies were a glamorous business…

Hardly surprising, perhaps, that she strove to break away from this trollop-typecasting by appearing in martial arts fantasy adventures – *Flying Daggers*, *Slave To The Sword* (1993) – but despite acquitting herself reasonably well in the arena of high-kicking hi-jinks, the roles on offer were hardly substantial enough to

Pauline Chan strikes a very politically incorrect pose with friend in The Girls From China

A sublime Pauline Chan in full fantasy mode

make her name in that field. *A Sudden Love*, Chan's one attempt at producing, was a piece of slushy romantic hokum, fifty percent story fifty percent Filipino travelogue, that vanished upon release. So, faced with a film career offering nothing more than endless hooker roles and the unsavoury prospect of becoming mixed up in more z-grade dross like *Haunting Evil Spirit* (1993) – that's the one with the rapist-repelling panties, bad taste fans! – Chan decided to turn her back on celluloid for good, citing the pressure of the business and the strain caused by her being ripped off by those of her circle she had entrusted to handle her financial affairs. Allied to those factors was her claim to be stepping aside for newer, fresher stars like Yung Hung (see elsewhere in this book). It is a claim with some conviction, as Yung immediately stepped into those hooker roles

PAULINE-ography

陳寶蓮

1991	Erotic Ghost Story 3
	Don Huang Tales of the Night
1992	Escape From Brothel
	The Girls From China
	Queen of the Underworld
	Behind the Pink Door
	A Wild Party
	Ladies From Shanghai
	Rogues From the North
	Girls Without Tomorrow
1993	Flying Daggers
	Devil of Rape
	A Sudden Love
	Spider Force
	Slave to the Sword
	Haunting Evil Spirit
	Sex For Sale
	He Born To Kill
	Who Cares
1994	From Beijing With Love
1996	Hong Kong Showgirls
	Once Upon a Time in Triad Society

Trust me I'm a doctor says
Waise Lee to Pauline

and *Who Cares* (all 1993) made use of leftover scenes from earlier movies to exploit Chan's name and reputation. The former actually excelled itself in managing to make two films out of one, so intense was the demand for Pauline in action. In Hong Kong, exploitation is no different from anywhere else!

Chan's subsequent career has been veiled in confusion. 1994 saw her make an as-yet fleeting screen return as the arch-villainess with missile-firing bra (!) in the Chow Sing Chi 007 spoof *From Beijing With Love*, but whether that heralded a full-time recommitment to celluloid remained unknown. As with several of her fellow Cat III leading ladies, she was still striving to get that singing career, the one she set her sights upon from an early age, off the ground. Whether audiences will take to the fully-clothed chanteuse Chan as readily as they did to the leggy libertine in skirts up to there will be interesting to see – and it could be some time coming, as Chan has reportedly been embroiled in contractual kerfuffles ever since. This could have been the reason she has made periodic returns to the screen in recent years, her latest being *Hong Kong Showgirls*, a Cantonese rehash of Paul Verhoeven's 1995 stinker *Showgirls*. Pauline's presence ensured a modicum of success for this Cat III exploitationer, demonstrating that, even if the singing has stalled, there will always be audiences out there who have a soft spot (or otherwise) for the charms of Pauline Chan Bo Lin…

From Beijing With Love

in which Chan had made her name – though now (and was this something Pauline saw coming?) the parts demanded an even greater degree of explicitness than even she – veteran of *Escape From Brothel* – had known. However, even this decision didn't prevent a rash of product supposedly 'starring' Pauline Chan in Cat III action hitting the streets. Shoddy product such as *Sex For Sale*, *Spider Force* (1992, released '93) *Devil Of Rape* (aka *Devil Of Love*), *He Born To Kill*

'many cruel and sexy stories...'

yung hung

My Pale Lover

suffer for your art

text:
Howard Lake

If 1993 failed to to produce a major Cat III hit on a par with *Sex and Zen* or *Naked Killer*, Wong Jing, exploitation producer supreme, soon remedied matters by unleashing upon the world *A Chinese Torture Chamber* (1994), a tour de force of extravagant madness which struck big with local audiences and whose global cult following is increasing even as we speak.

And it's understandable, for *A Chinese Torture Chamber* is a film unlike any other. Even the original historical romp, *Sex and Zen*, pales beside its intoxicating and total lack of restraint. The viewer has the feeling Wong Jing simply assembled his cast and crew and told them to do what the hell they

Yung Hung endures the traditional punishment for adultery in *A Chinese Torture Chamber*

翁虹

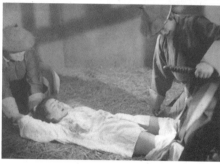

One thing leads to another... A Chinese Torture Chamber

A revealing Yung Hung

liked, however depraved or deranged things got. The result was a triumph for Wong Jing, not to mention a career-boosting tour de force for its female lead and Cat III sensation of 1994, Yung Hung, a petite beauty who has burst on to the scene in a big way since winning the 1991 Miss Asia beauty pageant. In essence, the movie is nothing more than a medieval sex comedy, but one doubts whether Robin Askwith would recognize it as such. Indeed, it's difficult to remind yourself just what kind of movie this is meant to be as slapstick, carnal japes – including a high-speed, wire-flying coupling that simply beggars belief – and exploding penises career by in between scenes of excruciating torture as an innocent village lass (Yung Hung) and her lover stand trial for the murder of the girl's husband. As the title forewarns, extracting a confession can be torture – literally, and in case you weren't quite certain, then we're treated to a fascinating (and painfully thorough) rundown on practically every method of judicial coercion popular in the Ching Dynasty – and, as we are assured in the pre-titles voiceover, every fiendish device has been meticulously researched in the quest for total authenticity.

A Chinese Torture Chamber once more had the outlandish and outrageous running amok at the top of the Hong Kong box office, with a two-month run in local theatres and further success abroad. For Yung Hung, it represented a consolidation of her pole position among the beauties of Cat III cinema (Pauline Chan

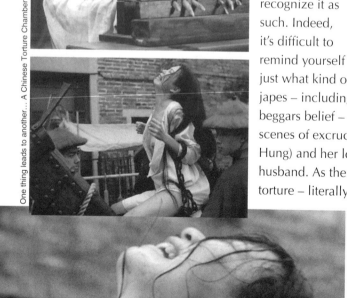

More agony and ecstacy… A Chinese Torture Chamber

claimed Hung's rise was one of the reasons she retired!), a position she has worked hard for with roles in *Don't Stop My Crazy Love For You* (1993), *Romance Of The Vampires*, *Guns of the Dragon*, *A Chinese Torture Chamber 2* (aka *Sex And The Emperor*) and *Ancient Chinese Whorehouse* (all 1994). It hasn't all been a bed of roses for Hung, however. Her Cat III scenes so offended the Yan Mei Club, an exclusive coterie of past beauty pageant winners, that they showed her the door, while her decision, upon winning the Miss Asia crown, to slate her predecessor Veronica Yip for making Cat III pictures was proven somewhat ill-advised once Hung's own raunchy career was underway. As we go to print her future seems in some doubt – a move from Cat III to less risque Cat II projects – *Dances With Dragons*, *Freedom Run Q*, *Fatal Obsession* (all '94) – has not reaped dividends and by September 1994 she was calling press conferences and tearfully explaining how much she regretted baring all for lurid shockers like *A Chinese Torture Chamber*. Alas, however, by then every sleazefiend in Hong Kong had bought the ticket, seen it and left with a glow as profound as Yung Hung's backside after the infamous 'paddlewhacking' scene.

Despite a rough ride with the censors (or

possibly as a result of same; after all, a cachet of notoriety has never been anathema to film marketing departments), *A Chinese Torture Chamber* delivered returns on a scale healthy enough for Wong Jing's Workshop to rattle off three (to date) sequels. *A Chinese Torture Chamber 2* aka *Sex And The Emperor* (1994) is the only one to have gained wider circulation at time of writing and it shows Wong Jing toning down the excesses of the original and opting more for an orthodox raunchy romp based on the premise that a chap in charge of the emperor's concubines could conceal that fact he was not made as

YUNG-ography
Yung Hung / Yvonne Yung

1993   My Virgin (cameo)
           Don't Stop My Crazy Love For You
1994   A Chinese Torture Chamber
           Freedom Run Q
           Guns of the Dragon
           Romance of the Vampires
           Bloody Fever
           Ancient Chinese Whorehouse
           Dances with Dragons
           Fatal Obsession
           Sex and the Emperor

翁虹

other eunuchs and was still in possession of fully-functioning nuptial apparatus without getting the chop, either from his job or, erm, the other way. There's a modicum of cruel and antisocial treatment meted out in a lacklustre kind of way, mostly directed toward Yung Hung, who, after the original and the sequel might have reason to decry her venture into Cat III – on the grounds of inhumane treatment of a leading lady if nothing else! – that satisfies the requirement of the film's title, but overall *A Chinese Torture Chamber 2* about passes muster as a bawdy period piece, though yet again the suspicion lingers that censors have had their wicked way with the

movie's lustier moments.

Whether or not Wong Jing made a conscious decision to draw back from including too many scenes which might set the fingers of moral guardians twitching for their scissors is difficult to tell. Producers in Hong Kong are not renowned for seeking confrontation with the powers that be – in a territory where box office performance will always rank way ahead of aesthetic integrity and battling for the purity of the director's 'vision', it is far easier to compromise and rake in the ackers than make a defiant stand over whether or not the whipping scene is 'artistically necessary' and crucial to the development of the plot.

However, it seems fairly certain we have seen the last of Yung Hung in these kinds of roles – and who can blame her? As a means of grabbing the spotlight and a huge slice of notoriety, her Cat III career has been a complete success. Yet, having matured a little and had time to reflect upon that 'success', she may have decided that, given a chance to do it again, she would heed advice from anybody but Wong Jing. Only time will tell whether Yung Hung has what it takes to leave her Cat III past behind and become a major star in more tasteful features. At present she has temporarily retired from making movies. Then again, given her canon to date, one is left with the overwhelming thought: how do you follow that..?

The lady is a vamp... Yung Hung in Romance of the Vampires

index

Ong, Judy:	202	Wong, Pauline:	181, 205
Oshima, Yukari:	11, 52, 54-57, 60-62, 64-73, 111, 115, 118, 187-188, 203, 210, 217, 219	Wu Chien Lien:	161
		Yang Chin Chin:	196
Pak Ka Shin:	185	Yang Hui Shan:	165
Pan Yin Tze:	202	Yau, Chingamy:	11, 180-181, 215, 220, 232-239, 241, 244
Pang Dang:	181		
Reis, Michelle:	11, 160, 184	Yeh, Sally:	7, 11, 131, 186-187
Rothrock, Cynthia:	52, 66, 68, 72, 97, 105, 118, 151, 203	Yeng Kim Fei:	16-17
		Yeoh, Michelle:	11, 55, 68, 71-72, 74-77, 96-103, 105, 107-108, 141
Shang Kwan, Polly:	35-40		
Shaw May Chi:	202	Yeung, Charlie:	165
Shih Szu:	21-23	Yeung Pan Pan:	9, 40-45, 68, 70
Shiomi, Sue:	65, 188	Yeung, Pauline:	199
Siu, Josephene:	157-158	Yi Suk Kwan:	202
Sydney:	202	Yip, Amy:	7, 8, 11, 151, 166, 168, 170, 173, 184-185, 207, 215, 218, 220-231, 233, 235, 244
Tai Yau Lay Choi:	213		
Tien Niu:	52, 182		
Ting Pei, Betty:	28, 193		
Tsui Ho Ying:	183	Yip, Cecilia:	170, 216
Tso Yung:	209	Yip, Francoise:	201
Wan, Irene:	177	Yip, Gloria:	177
Wang Ping:	194	Yip, Veronica:	11, 166, 253
Wen, Candy:	196	Yu Li:	176
Wong Chiu Yin:	202	Yuan Chu:	198
Wong, Faye:	162, 169	Yuen, Anita:	162
Wong Hang Sau:	191	Yuen, Fennie:	202
		Yuen Man:	208
Wong, Joey:	8, 11, 85, 101, 120-127, 132, 160, 168	Yung Hung:	215, 218-219, 249-254

recommended viewing

(A SELECTION OF UK VIDEO RELEASES WITH A FIGHTING FEMMES SLANT WORTH CHECKING OUT)

A MOMENT OF ROMANCE
Wu Chien Lien
Made in Hong Kong, cert 18

AN EYE FOR AN EYE
Joey Wong
TVB/Eastern Heroes, cert 18

ANGEL
Elaine Liu, Moon Lee, Yukari Oshima
M.I.A./Hong Kong Classics, cert 18

ANGEL 2
Moon Lee
M.I.A./Hong Kong Classics, cert 18

ANGEL ENFORCERS
Yeung Pan Pan
M.I.A./Hong Kong Classics, cert 18

AVENGING QUARTET
Yukari Oshima, Michiko Nishiwaki,
Moon Lee, Cynthia Khan
M.I.A./Hong Kong Classics, cert 18

BLACK CAT
Jade Leung
Made in Hong Kong, cert 18

BRAVE YOUNG GIRLS
Yukari Oshima, Hui Ying Hung
TVB/Eastern Heroes, cert 18

CHUNGKING EXPRESS
Faye Wong, Brigitte Lin,
Chow Kar Ling
ICA Projects, cert 12

CITY COPS
aka BEYOND THE LAW
Michiko Nishiwaki, Cynthia Rothrock
M.I.A./Hong Kong Classics, cert 18

DEADLY CHINA DOLLS
Sibelle Hu, Maria Jo, Miyamoto Yoko
Eastern Heroes, cert 18

DEADLY DREAM WOMAN
Chingamy Yau, Cheung Man,
Deannie Ip
Eastern Heroes, cert 18

DEADLY TARGET
Yukari Oshima, Yeung Pan Pan
TVB/Eastern Heroes, cert 18

DREAMING THE REALITY
Yukari Oshima, Moon Lee,
Sibelle Hu
Eastern Heroes, cert 18

EROTIC CHINA DOLLS
aka DANCES WITH SNAKES
Fan Li Chi, Hsu Meng Wah, Cat III
Eastern Heroes, cert 18

ESCAPE FROM BROTHEL
Pauline Chan, Rena Murakami, Cat III
Eastern Heroes, cert 18

FORCE OF THE DRAGON
aka IN THE LINE OF DUTY 3
Cynthia Khan
Imperial Entertainment, cert 18

GHOSTLY LOVE
Hui Tien Chee, Emily Chu, Cat III
Eastern Heroes, cert 18

GUARDIAN ANGEL
Yukari Oshima
TVB/Eastern Heroes, cert 18

HEROIC TRIO, THE
Maggie Cheung, Michelle Yeoh,
Anita Mui
Made in Hong Kong, cert 18

HEROIC TRIO 2: EXECUTIONERS
Maggie Cheung, Michelle Yeoh,
Anita Mui
Made in Hong Kong, cert 18

HONG KONG GIGOLO
Carina Lau, Cat III
TVB/Eastern Heroes, cert 18

IN THE LINE OF DUTY
aka WITNESS
Cynthia Khan
Imperial Entertainment, cert 18

LETHAL PANTHER
Yukari Oshima
Eastern Heroes, cert 15

MIDDLE MAN
Cynthia Khan
TVB/Eastern Heroes, cert 18

MIDNIGHT ANGEL
Yukari Oshima, May Law,
Leung Wan Yui
Eastern Heroes, cert 18

MOON WARRIORS
Maggie Cheung, Anita Mui
Made in Hong Kong, cert 18

MY YOUNG AUNTIE
Hui Ying Hung
Made in Hong Kong, cert 15

NAKED KILLER
Chingamy Yau, Carrie Ng
Uncut collector's box set available
M.I.A./Hong Kong Classics, cert 18

NOCTURNAL DEMON
Moon Lee
TVB/Eastern Heroes, cert 18

OTHER SIDE OF THE SEA, THE
Michelle Reis
TVB/Eastern Heroes, cert 18

OUTLAW BROTHERS
Yukari Oshima
M.I.A./Hong Kong Classics, cert 18

PINK BOMB
Cynthia Khan
TVB/Eastern Heroes, cert 15

POLICE ASSASSINS 2
aka YES MADAM
Michelle Yeoh
Screen Entertainment, cert 18

PRINCESS MADAM
Moon Lee, Michiko Nishiwaki,
Yeung Pan Pan
M.I.A./Hong Kong Classics, cert 18

REVENGE OF ANGEL
Moon Lee
TVB/Eastern Heroes, cert PG

SAVIOUR OF THE SOUL
Anita Mui, Gloria Yip
Made in Hong Kong, cert 15

TIGER CAGE 2
Rosamund Kwan, Cynthia Khan
Made in Hong Kong, cert 18

TOP SQUAD
**aka THE INSPECTOR WEARS
A SKIRT**
Cynthia Rothrock, Sibelle Hu
Imperial Entertainment, cert 18

TWO WONDROUS TIGERS
Yeung Pan Pan
*Eastern Heroes/Imperial
Entertainment, 15*

WIDOW WARRIORS
Hui Ying Hung, Michiko Nishiwaki,
Elizabeth Lee, Tien Niu
TVB/Eastern Heroes, cert 18

WING CHUN
Michelle Yeoh
Made in Hong Kong, cert 12

FILMED INTERVIEWS:

TOP FIGHTER
Yukari Oshima
Eastern Heroes, cert 18

**EASTERN HEROES VIDEO
MAGAZINE 1**
Moon Lee, Yukari Oshima
Eastern Heroes, cert 18

**EASTERN HEROES VIDEO
MAGAZINE 2**
Yeung Pan Pan
Eastern Heroes, cert 18

**All titles are available from
the Eastern Heroes shop or
by mail order from
Interactive Mail**